KAYAKING *The New Whitewater Sport for Everybody*

KAYAKING

The New Whitewater Sport for Everybody

BY **JAY EVANS**
former U.S. Olympic Coach
AND **ROBERT R. ANDERSON**

THE STEPHEN GREENE PRESS *Brattleboro, Vermont*

This book has been produced in the United States of America: designed by Irving Perkins, composed by American Book–Stratford Press, and printed by The Murray Printing Co.

It is published by the Stephen Greene Press, Brattleboro, Vermont 05301.

Illustration Credits
The following photographers and artists contributed illustrations for this book: Robert R. Anderson, Robert F. George, Klepper-Werke Photo, Chris Knight, Kolivas Photo, Ledyard Canoe Club, Old Town Canoe Company, U.S. National Museum, Neil Quinn, Walter Richardson, and John T. Urban. The name or initials of the contributor appears at the end of each illustration caption. Frontispiece by John T. Urban.

Many of the persons in the illustrations are dedicated amateur athletes, who neither sought nor received any remuneration or benefit for allowing photographs of themselves to be used in this book. J.E.

Library of Congress Cataloging in Publication Data
Evans, Jay, 1925–
   Kayaking.
   1. Canoes and canoeing. 2. White-water canoe-
ing. I. Anderson, Robert R., 1942–   joint au-
thor. II. Title.
GV783.E94   797.1′22   73-82750
ISBN 0-8289-0208-9
ISBN 0-8289-0192-9 pbk.

77 78 79 80 81 9 8 7 6 5 4 3

PUBLISHED MAY 1975
Second printing October 1975
Third printing May 1977

Contents

Silhouetted against flatwater, a kayaker practices maneuvering through slalom gates. (L.C.C.)

1 *The Lure of Whitewater*
[J . E .]

WATER is a fascinating thing. Next to the air we breathe it is probably the most significant thing on this planet. Certainly there is more of it around than any other material, for three fourths of the earth's surface is covered with it, and over 80 percent of the human body consists of it. It is the universal fluid: we drink it plain, or we doctor it up by adding color, flavor and gas to it. We use it to create power and light for growing food, washing our clothes, mining for rare metals, and transporting goods from here to there.

Of all the substances on earth, water has some of the most interesting characteristics. First of all, it is wet and slippery. It slithers around unless penned up, and it works tirelessly to escape its bonds so it can rush downhill until it eventually joins the ocean. If dammed up it will quietly bide its time and then descend as rain somewhere else on earth in its relentless journey to the sea.

Fresh water is quite heavy, weighing about 62 pounds per cubic foot. This means that in addition to having the quality of weight, it can create a lot of force. The kayaker discovers this when he tries to dislodge his boat from a rock in the rapids: water can exert 8 to 10 tons of force against a boat hung up in a fast-moving current.

Water also has personality. It appears alive. It can sparkle; it can look ominous. Its gentle sound can lull you to sleep, its boisterousness can tingle your nerves, or its forbidding roar can fill your heart with apprehension.

Water is incredibly versatile. As a liquid it is most common, but as a solid it can cool you off on a hot day or store itself up for the spring run-off. As a crystal it gives birth to the world of skiing, tobogganing, snowshoeing, and snowmobiling. As a solid it can be skated upon.

Water, as a liquid, is dynamic. It can form the tiniest ripple from a trout nibbling on the surface of a quiet pond, or become a 50-foot tidal wave roaring across the wide expanse of the Pacific Ocean.

One of the greatest moments in the history of mankind must have been when man first discovered that he could move in water either by swimming himself or by riding along on a log. Together with the invention of the wheel and the use of fire and metal, man's ability to propel himself along in water marked a major breakthrough in the development of civilization. No longer landlocked, man had a whole new horizon extending before him, much as space travel in our own age now lures us on to the distant stars.

And as he mastered water, he learned to play in it. Actually, there are only two ingredients necessary to enjoy boating on water: an ability to swim reasonably well with confidence, and an appreciation of and fondness for water—even if it is cold. If you enjoy the smell and touch of water and are fascinated by moving current and thrilled at the sight of rapids, then perhaps kayaking is for you.

In general, people of all ages enjoy kayaking. Children just barely big enough to see over the cockpit and strong enough to lift a paddle have been seen kayaking merrily around millponds and gentle streams. Historically, the Eskimos began to teach their children the Eskimo Roll as soon as the child had reached the age of 12.

In terms of muscular co-ordination, experience has shown that youngsters of 8 and 9 often have a remarkable sense of balance and movement and can handle themselves smartly in the water. Of course the fact that these little folk probably weigh only 60 pounds or less certainly gives them an advantage, for with so little weight in the boat it rests as lightly on the water as a leaf, and seems able to turn at a mere suggestion.

During the adolescent years and in the 20's those who enjoy kayaking will often be caught in the competitive urge, will turn more serious about the sport, and will train their bodies to a fine pitch to improve their skill. Many schools, colleges and youth groups are taking up kayaking as an ideal environmental sport.

Perhaps the golden years of kayaking extend from age 30 to 60.

To an experienced paddler, frothing whitewater is an invitation to an exhilarating, challenging run. (J.T.U.)

By the time a person is 35 (if he is realistic about himself) he will no longer try to keep up with the college crowd to win the coveted racing championship, but will gladly settle for the veteran or senior racing class. And many more will be content simply to attend a race, sharing the excitement that prevails in the campground and taking part in the activities.

Older people should not shy away from kayaking either. Steering your own little craft around the coves and inlets of a wilderness pond, in search of fish or wildfowl or even an illusive view of a sunset, can be a rewarding experience. If, gliding along silently, you round a bend and suddenly come upon a deer—or better yet, a moose or an elk—the day will long be remembered.

A well-known set of rapids that has given you many good times in past years will always welcome you again as a long-lost friend. And what can be more satisfying than introducing a young paddler for the first time to one of your favorite whitewater runs?

As therapy, kayaking is unmatched in its ability to wash away the pressures of a too highly charged modern society. A weekend trip, or even a Sunday afternoon paddle, can rejuvenate your spirits for a taxing week ahead.

Thoreau was right: rivers are a constant lure to the adventurous instinct in mankind.

2 The Boats
[R . R . A .]

IN THIS CHAPTER we take a look at the evolution of the kayak and its cousin, the closed-deck canoe, describe the modern kayaks, and offer pointers on how to choose the right boat for you.

FROM NANOOK TO THE OLYMPICS

The native North Americans developed three unique species of boat: the dugout canoe used in the warmer climates; the birchbark canoe used in the great northern forest region; and the skin boat used in the barren Arctic. The arctic boats were fundamental to life in the harsh world from the Bering Sea to the east coast of Greenland.

Easily the best known of the arctic skin boats is the kayak. Originally a hunting boat, its closed deck and sealed cockpit kept the hunter warm, and made the kayak seaworthy in rough water. Its streamlined shape made it fast through the sea and easy to paddle. Typical dimensions—about 18 feet in length and 1½ feet across the beam—made it even longer and narrower than today's recreational kayaks. Double-bladed paddles were common, although some single-bladed paddles were used.

The unique construction of the kayak made it resilient and durable in wild, ice-filled seas. The kayak frame was a masterpiece of primitive engineering. The supporting member was not the keel, as it is in most wood-boat construction, but the gunwale. A framework

11

Two Eskimos in a skin kayak were photographed near Nunivak Island, Alaska, in the early 1900's. The hole in the bow is a built-in grabloop. Note the unusual single-bladed paddle. Most tribes used double-bladed paddles with the blades in the same plane, unlike modern paddles with blades set at right angles. (U.S. NATIONAL MUSEUM)

of bent staves was hung from the gunwale and lashed to battens running fore and aft. The bow end, and sometimes the stern as well, was extended to provide a handgrip for lifting the kayak from the sea. The deck was built like the hull, but could be structurally less robust since the deck did not get the same kind of abuse as the hull. Sealskin was used to cover the kayak frame, and seal sinews lashed the frame together. The skin was stretched taut, but because it was not sewn to the frame, collision with a chunk of ice was less likely to cause a tear.

The hunter drew the bottom of his parka over the cockpit rim, fastening it with a drawstring. Thus buttoned in, if he capsized he could roll up without shipping water.

Beginning as a Sport

Kayaking for sport developed in southern Germany around the turn of the century. Lured by the whitewater rivers rising high in the nearby Alps, people began to experiment with wood-framed, fabric-covered boats based on the Eskimo kayak. Out of the experimentation came the collapsible kayak—*das Faltboot*. The frame was assembled on the riverbank and inserted into a fabric outer skin. When the day's boating was over, the *Faltboot* could be quickly disassembled.

By the time World War II broke out, whitewater competition, the distant cousin of flatwater racing, was well developed. Flatwater kayak racing won a place in the 1936 Olympic Games. The first world championship whitewater slalom race was held in 1949 in Switzerland, and in 1955 the first wildwater (downriver) world championship (time trials through rapids) was held in conjunction with the slalom competition.

Whitewater slalom racing began officially in the United States in 1952 on the Brandywine River in Delaware. Early slalom races were typically run in open canoes with a smattering of *Faltboots* in attendance. In 1958, the first national championship slalom trials were held on Vermont's West River.

The Fiberglass Revolution

In the mid-Fifties, innovators began experimenting with fiber-reinforced plastic (commonly called fiberglass) for making kayaks. A revolution followed. The new material permitted the development of new types of boats that were stronger, lighter, and more maneuverable. This in turn made new boating techniques possible, and rapids that had been dismissed as impossible were now run with ease.

Almost all the early boats were homemade, but by the end of the decade, manufacturers and designers were producing strong, responsive fiberglass craft. In the early Seventies the sport reached maturity, and whitewater slalom was accepted as a new event in the 1972 Munich Olympics.

ANATOMY OF A FIBERGLASS KAYAK

The modern fiberglass kayak is a simple boat—a deck, a hull, a seat, a pair of grabloops, and a bracing system for the paddler. There is no internal framework. The kayak varies in length between a little over 13 feet to a little under 15 feet. Width is about 2 feet. Draft—

the portion of the hull under the waterline—is only a couple of inches. Over-all height is rarely more than 1½ feet; weight is about 25 to 35 pounds.

Fiberglass is used in both slalom and wildwater (downriver) craft, the basic designs of which will be fully described later.

The one-man kayak (K–1 in paddling jargon), has only a few parts, but all are fundamental to its performance. The hull and the deck are discussed later in terms of boat types as they are basic to determining handling characteristics. Nevertheless, let's take a brief look now.

THE HULL

The fiberglass hull is molded in one piece. There is no keel. The shape of the hull is the single most important factor in how the kayak behaves. It is usually built to be a little heavier and more durable than the deck, which does not get the same banging around in whitewater. A seam of fiberglass tape joins the hull to the deck.

THE DECK

The purpose of the deck is to keep water out of the boat, not, as some of the uninitiated suspect, to keep the paddler in. Therefore it is higher in the middle so that water will run off. Like the hull, the deck is molded in one piece of fiberglass. Roughly in the center of the deck is the cockpit hole, and at both ends there is a hole through which the grabloop fits.

THE SEAT

The seat is part of an integrally molded fiberglass unit which includes the cockpit rim (coaming) and the hipbraces. The seat hangs from the cockpit ½ inch or so above the hull so the hull can flex when running over a submerged rock. Most manufacturers add chocks of ethafoam between the hipbraces and the sides of the hull to keep the seat from shifting when the paddler leans hard over to one side.

Some kayaks come equipped with a lower-back support, an adjustable, broad strap that attaches to the hipbraces.

A fiberglass seat hangs from the cockpit of a kayak (the bow end is at the bottom of the photograph). A woven strap supports the kayaker's back; his knees press against the molded braces on either side. The wooden rod beneath the seat and the styrofoam chock wedged behind the seat help stiffen the kayak. The spray-skirt fits over the coaming that rims the cockpit. (R.F.G.)

THE COAMING

The coaming is the convex lip around the cockpit, and is part of the seat unit. The elasticized edge of the spray-skirt fits over the coaming and stops water from entering through the cockpit.

THE GRABLOOPS

At either end of the kayak there is a grabloop. The grabloop offers a grip in retrieving a capsized kayak. When fastening the kayak to the top of a car, a line can be run from the grabloops to the car's bumpers to secure the boat.

THE BRACING SYSTEM

The bracing system consists of hip-, knee-, and footbraces. The bracing system is the heart of modern kayaking, for it permits the paddler to "wear" the kayak rather than just to sit in it. To brace yourself in the kayak you simply press against the foot- and knee-braces.

People unfamiliar with the modern kayak invariably fear being trapped in the kayak while upside down in the water. Actually, this

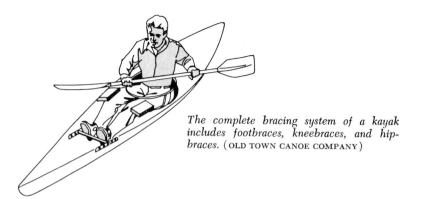

The complete bracing system of a kayak includes footbraces, kneebraces, and hipbraces. (OLD TOWN CANOE COMPANY)

is impossible. When you release your pressure against the foot- and kneebraces and give an easy tug to free the spray-skirt from the coaming, gravity allows you to slip out of the kayak and swim free.

Footbraces

There are two common types of footbraces: crossbar and pedal. Footbraces on commercially produced kayaks have several possible fore and aft positions to accommodate a variety of leg lengths. Many a home builder positions the footbraces permanently if he is to be the only user.

Both bracing systems have their advocates. The argument for the bar brace is that it allows the feet to slide laterally yet still maintain contact with the bar. The paddlers who prefer pedal braces feel they are safer because pedal braces are less of an obstruction when the feet are suddenly withdrawn.

Kneebraces

The kayak is designed so that the knees press against the inside of the deck. Some decks are contoured to accommodate the knees; others have specially molded kneebraces attached to the deck. Manufacturers usually glue foam pads in the kneebrace area for comfort.

Hipbraces

Hipbraces are really just the sides of the seat, usually contoured to accept the fullness of the hip. Hipbraces work in conjunction with the seat to prevent the paddler from sliding around. Unlike foot- and kneebraces, which you must press against to maintain contact, hipbraces require no effort on your part.

TYPES OF KAYAKS

To the inexperienced eye, most kayaks look alike—long, slender plastic tubes. You have to know something about them to recognize the subtle contour changes that make a great difference in the handling characteristics.

There are two basic types of kayaks: slalom and downriver. The latter type is designated as *wildwater* in the terminology of the International Canoe Federation, the world-wide governing body for kayak competition. (Although "downriver" seems more descriptive to North American boaters, we will be using "wildwater" throughout this book in order to be consistent with ICF language, which here comes from the German *Wildwasser.*) Both types of kayak correspond in concept to Alpine skiing's slalom and downhill racing.

A slalom kayak is designed for paddling at top speed through a series of "gates" situated along a stretch of rapids. Obviously, the boat's ability to turn responsively in turbulent water is the prime essential for a well-designed slalom kayak.

Wildwater kayaks race in a time-trial from Point A in the rapids to Point B some miles downstream. Straight-ahead speed is what wins a slam-bang race down the river, plus just enough maneuverability so obstructions in the river can be avoided.

A recreational kayak can partake of the characteristics of either type of racing boat, or any design that suits the owner's liking and purpose.

Slalom Kayaks

Slalom kayaks must be no shorter than 13 feet 2 inches (4 meters) or narrower than 23¾ inches (60 centimeters) to meet International Canoe Federation regulations, which put these limits on design in order to emphasize paddling skill.

Seen in sideways profile, the most noticeable feature of a slalom kayak is the pronounced "rocker," the upward-sweeping curvature of the hull at either end. Turn the slalom kayak upside down and

Slalom kayak, left, and the longer wildwater kayak, right. Both have the same maximum width by ICF rules. However, the slalom kayak maintains the width over much of its length to gain stability, whereas the wildwater kayak is as narrow as possible for straight-ahead speed. (N.Q.)

it displays another characteristic: a broad, flat bottom. Without a keel to keep it running straight, the slalom boat quickly—and maddeningly to the newcomer to paddling—turns itself broadside. The bow end of the slalom kayak hull usually has a minimal V shape to give it a little tracking (or straight-ahead) capability.

Volume defined

The over-all shape of the slalom kayak—and to a lesser extent that of wildwater and recreational kayaks—is defined in terms of its volume. Kayaks that meet the same ICF regulations may be either high or low volume. To simplify, imagine two balloons, one inflated more than the other. Stuff both balloons into identical shoe boxes. One takes up more room in the box than the other—thus we get high volume or low volume.

The high-volume kayak is fuller. The deck is higher over more of its surface, the sides are like gently rounded slabs, and the maximum width is carried over much of the waterline.

The low-volume kayak is sometimes called a "pumpkin seed." It has a virtually flat deck and the sides come to a sharp edge. The maximum width at the waterline is a good deal less than that of a high-volume kayak.

VOLUME AND PERFORMANCE

It should be noted that low-volume slalom kayaks are generally intended to be quick boats that can make sharp turns, even while tilted up and riding on edge. These kayaks require good body balance as well as some getting-used-to. They are used for racing on moderate whitewater rivers.

For heavier paddlers and for courses with very rough water, the more buoyant and stable high-volume designs are a better choice. Their behavior is slower but generally steadier, good for both competitive and recreational paddling. And because of their rounder sides, high-volume boats are easier to Eskimo Roll than the flatter low-volume designs: after all, in the breakfast frying pan the sausage flips easier than the flapjack.

Wildwater (Downriver) Kayaks

Wildwater (downriver) kayaks, like slalom kayaks, must conform to ICF regulations. The wildwater kayak may be no more than

The keel of the slalom kayak is curved, allowing it to pivot easily; the wildwater kayak has a flat keel to facilitate use of the Forward stroke. (N.Q.)

The slalom kayak's wide, flat bottom promotes stability, and the rounded sides permit the boat to be leaned on edge without losing control. (N.Q.)

The wildwater kayak's maximum width occurs above the waterline, sacrificing stability but gaining in speed from the slender, V-shaped hull. (N.Q.)

14 feet 8 inches (4.5 meters) long and at least 23¾ inches (60 centimeters) wide.

This kayak is a long, narrow boat because a long, narrow boat is fast (as opposed to slalom kayaks, which are short because short, round-bottom boats turn easily and quickly).

The wildwater kayak is rakish in appearance, fast but tippy in performance. Like a bicycle, it is stable at speed and increasingly unstable as the speed drops.

Seen in bow-to-stern profile, the bottom of the hull is virtually flat with just enough upsweep at bow and stern to ride over submerged rocks and to provide some turning capability. Cross-sectioned, the hull has a rounded V shape that tapers to an extremely sharp bow and stern. This long, wedge-shaped hull slips through the water and, by providing good resistance to turning, makes efficient use of the Forward paddle stroke.

Seen head-on, the wildwater kayak tapers from a butter-knife-on-edge bow to its broadest point just behind the cockpit. From that widest point, it tapers in a quick sweep to the stern. Unlike the bow of the slalom kayak, the knife-like bow will slice through standing waves.

Recreational Kayaks

Most recreational kayaks are based on the slalom racing kayak, in many cases even conforming to ICF regulations for slalom length and width. The recreational kayak of the slalom type usually has a high-volume design to increase stability and provide more interior room both for comfort and as storage space for duffle.

A few recreational kayaks are based on wildwater design, having the hull modified to give greater stability. The resulting shape is excellent for flatwater touring and fastwater runs. However, the essential turning limitation still persists.

Several manufacturers produce child-size kayaks based on the slalom design. With a length of only about 11 feet—roughly 2 feet shorter than ICF regulations—this kayak is easier to manage. Any child who can swim well can be allowed to paddle, although few children under the age of 10 can achieve actual control of a kayak.

DAS FALTBOOT—THE FOLDING KAYAK

The fiberglass revolution in whitewater kayaking spelled the end of the folding kayak as a competitive boat. It did not, however, mean the end of the folding kayak for other purposes. Despite the emergence and general availability of fiberglass kayaks, there are still folks who run moderate whitewater rivers in folding kayaks. The major use of folding boats today is for flatwater cruising and camping, because they are larger, roomier, and more stable in the hands of casual paddlers than their fiberglass relatives.

The easiest way to understand the principle of the folding kayak is to think of a hinged shoe tree. Insert one end into the toe of the shoe, the other into the heel. Press down on the hinged shaft and the shoe tree becomes a rigid support for the shoe. The folding kayak's wood frame is assembled on the ground in two halves. Each half is inserted into the one-piece outer skin and the frame is sprung rigid and held with a snap-lock fitting.

The deck of the folding kayak is cotton; the hull is heavy fabric coated with vinyl. There is no bracing system. Cockpits are generous and the seat (or seats, for there is a two-person model) has a backrest. For the single paddler alone on a camping trip, the unused seat of the two-person model allows extra storage for camping gear. Flotation bags are provided; special spray-skirts, though available, are rarely used in flatwater. You can buy sailing equipment—aluminum mast, sails, rudder, and leeboards—for a folding boat.

The K–2

A few manufacturers produce fiberglass two-person kayaks. The K–2 is a recreational boat, generally based on the slalom shape with the paddlers sitting directly behind one another and positioned close together in the middle of the boat. Since there is no provision in the ICF rules for K–2 whitewater racing, the dimensions of K–2's are not regulated.

Unlike the closed-deck two-person canoe (C–2) which evolved from the great tradition of the Canadien canoe, the K–2 has no tradition behind it. There were some Eskimo kayak two-seaters but the traditional arctic kayak was a one-person boat. For this reason, and because there is no K–2 whitewater racing, the K–2 has not achieved much popularity.

The surfing kayak

A fiberglass surf kayak looks a lot like a well-worn bedroom slipper. The toe—in this case the bow—is blunt and has a slight upsweep. Although a slalom kayak can be used for surfing it tends to nosedive on steep waves. The upswept blunt bow of the surf kayak prevents this. The construction of the surf kayak is very similar to other fiberglass kayaks; it has a bracing system and requires a bow flotation bag. Its advantage over a surfboard is that it permits the paddler to get out from shore a lot quicker to catch another wave.

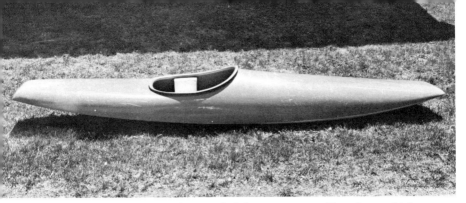

The fiberglass surf kayak is distinguished by its upswept, blunt bow, which helps prevent nosediving in steep waves. (R.F.G.)

THE FLATWATER RACING KAYAK AND CANOE

Flatwater racing kayaks and canoes are not within the scope of this book, but it would be an injustice not to note their existence. The flatwater racing boats are regulated by the ICF as to length and width, just as are whitewater racing boats. Kayak competitions are for singles, pairs, and fours; canoe competitions are for singles and pairs.

Most flatwater boats are molded plywood, although some are fiberglass. The rules state that kayaks may have steering rudders; canoes may have keels. The basic shape is very similar to that of the wildwater kayak—extremely narrow with the widest point just behind the cockpit for good tracking. The wildwater kayak, in fact, is based on these boats.

The Whitewater Canoe

It is impossible to mention whitewater kayaks and ignore the whitewater closed-deck canoe. In whitewater racing, as you will later discover, there are classes for both kayaks and closed-deck canoes.

C–1

The fiberglass closed-deck one-person canoe (designated as the C–1) is often mistaken for a kayak. The giveaways are that the C–1 paddler uses a single-bladed paddle, and kneels rather than sits.

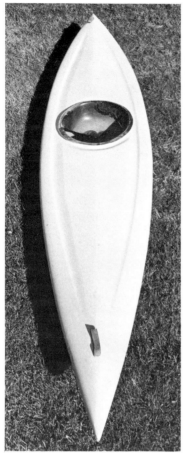

The C-1 slalom boat is similar in basic design to the K-1 slalom, though until 1973 ICF rules required the bow and stern to be the highest point on all canoes to preserve the traditional Canadien shape. (R.F.G.)

The C-1 wildwater boat is fundamentally the same in concept as the K-1 wildwater. Note how the designer cleverly complied with the ICF minimum-width rules while still keeping the shape as slender as possible. (L.C.C.)

The C–1 is raced in both slalom and wildwater competition. The basic principles of kayak design apply to canoe design. However, until a rule change in 1973, the highest point of both the C–1 and C–2 (two-person canoe, discussed in a minute) was required to be no further than 11⅘ inches (30 centimeters) from each end of the boat to preserve the traditional shape of the Canadien canoe. The C–1 slalom may be no shorter, by ICF regulations, than 13 feet 2 inches (4 meters—same as the slalom kayak) and at least 27½ inches wide (70 centimeters—3¾ inches wider than the slalom kayak). The downriver canoe must be no longer than 14 feet 1 inch (4.3 meters— 7 inches shorter than the downriver kayak) or narrower than 31½ inches (80 centimeters).

The concept of bracing is also applied in the design of these canoes. The paddler kneels on kneebraces with feet braced against toeblocks. Two straps run from the center of the hull floor to the side of the C–1, and against these the paddler braces the inside of the thighs. A small seat or strap is suspended from the coaming at the rear of the cockpit.

The paddling position puts the canoeist's eye level considerably higher than the kayaker's and therefore the canoeist has a more comprehensive view of the river. In paddling a canoe, you lean from the waist and to a lesser extent lean the canoe. Like the kayak, the C–1 can be Eskimo Rolled.

C–2

In whitewater racing the two-person closed-deck canoe (designated as C–2 or C–2M for mixed sexes) is the only two-person-in-one-boat category.

The paddlers in the slalom C–2 sit in line toward each end for better turning control. In the wildwater (downriver) C–2 they sit close together in the center of the boat, with the cockpits offset so the paddlers can make Forward strokes without an excessive sideways reach that would lessen their power.

The C–2 slalom must be 15 feet (4.58 meters) long and at least 31½ inches (80 centimeters) wide. The downriver C–2 must be no longer than 16 feet 4 inches (5 meters) and 31½ inches (80 centimeters) wide.

The C–2 slalom boat. *The seats are in line and near the ends of the boat for easier turning.* (R.F.G.)

The C–2 wildwater boat. *The seats are closer together but slightly offset so the paddlers can make the most powerful Forward strokes.* (R.F.G.)

Recreational C–2's are usually set up along slalom lines with a cargo hatch in the middle between the cockpits.

THE MATERIALS

Before we start, it is best to note that what is called a fiberglass kayak is mistakenly named. It should be called an "FRP" kayak since fiber-reinforced plastic is the most popular material for building these boats.

FRP

Without FRP (*fiber-reinforced plastic*), the sport of whitewater kayaking could not have reached its present level of maturity, for the resilience and versatility of this comparatively new material have combined to allow innovations in design that have, in turn, led to a revolution in paddling technique.

Not only is FRP resilient, it is also cheap and quick to work with experimentally. Thus it can be molded easily into virtually any shape in the creation of new kayak and canoe designs, permitting sharp edges and smooth and intricate contours that would be impractical —and sometimes impossible—in wood.

The basic components of FRP are fiberglass cloth, resin, and either a catalytic agent (if the resin is a polyester) or a co-reactive hardener (if the resin is an epoxy); most commercially manufactured kayaks employ the less toxic polyester resins. When the catalytic agent is added to polyester resin, an irreversible chemical process occurs. Heat will not return the resulting product to the sum of its parts nor will it permit reshaping. What's done is done.

Experimentation has proved that superior materials do not necessarily produce a superior result. Reason: the compatibility of the materials in combination with one another is more critical to the end product than the particular qualities of any of the component materials.

Fabrics

Fabrics used for kayaks are fiberglass cloth, which is sometimes combined with chopped fiberglass mat, and nylon and polypropylene cloth.

FIBERGLASS CLOTH

The fiberglass cloths most commonly used by home builders are 6-ounce or 10-ounce (per square yard) basket weave, available at many hardware and sporting goods stores. By contrast, commercial kayak manufacturers select from a range of hundreds of cloths, since fiberglass comes in a wide variety of weights, weaves, densities, filament combinations, and surface treatments.

Particular attention is paid to the cloth's weight, since a competition slalom kayak is expected to weigh not more than 25 pounds. More important yet is the ability of the cloth to grip the resin; whatever the other virtues of a particular cloth, unless it works well in combination with the resin the result will be inferior.

Chopped fiberglass mat is sometimes used in conjunction with fiberglass cloth to add stiffening and to achieve a better bond with the resin. It consists of fiberglass filaments laid at random like felt, and has little strength of its own.

NYLON AND POLYPROPYLENE

Nylon and polypropylene cloth have good flexibility and resist tearing well. When a boat crashes, these cloths help to hold together the broken pieces, but they have little dimensional stability and deform when heated by a hot sun.

Resin

Half to three quarters of a kayak's weight is resin. Resin is a goopy substance, essentially plastic in the liquid and uncured state. The plastics industry produces a variety of resins, some brittle, some flexible. Kayak resin must be flexible, but not so flexible that the kayak loses its shape. If it is too brittle—like the hardware-store type for home building—the impregnated fiberglass cloth will snap under impact. Most manufacturers modify available resins to achieve the balance they want.

Structural Supports for FRP

Lightweight FRP boats often need a little structural assistance. Styrofoam or ethafoam cut in slabs and jammed on edge help to preserve the shape of the design when the hull, or more typically the deck, has been built with insufficient structural strength. If this kind of support has been added, it does not mean the kayak is poorly built. It's just another solution.

Fiberglass tapes laid at intervals across the width of the inside of the deck also add stiffening.

Wooden rods—or more usually one narrow rod in the center of the hull running bow to stern beneath the seat and held in place with fiberglass cloth—stiffen the hull.

THE MANUFACTURING PROCESS

Fiberglass kayaks are made by hand, and the manufacturing process is essentially simple.

Several layers of fabric—which may be fiberglass cloth, mat, or synthetic cloths, depending on the builder's preference—are laid in open molds, one mold for the hull and one for the deck. The cloth in the molds is saturated with liquid resin. As the cloth cures in the mold, the waste is trimmed off flush with the edges of the mold.

Then the hull and deck molds are clamped together while a strip of saturated fiberglass tape is applied to the interior seam where the hull and deck join. The mold is removed and the coaming-hipbrace-seat unit is glued in place. Foot- and kneebraces are installed. Holes are drilled in the deck ends and the grabloops are drawn through and sealed in place with a dollop of resin.

Home-building

The beginner should be leery of trying it himself, for the drawbacks are significant. The special resins and cloth today considered essential to building are available by the drum and bolt—a healthy investment and absurdly impractical for constructing just one boat.

Finding someone with a mold may require a lot of investigation and even then the mold may not be for a boat that will suit you.

Working with plastics carries the risk of damage to your health—permanent damage—if you don't scrupulously observe industrial hygiene standards.

THE KITS

Several manufacturers offer kits for boats of a number of designs. A kit consists of a deck, hull, seat, and brace hardware. You have only to install the seat and braces, and seam the deck and hull together. If you are handy and follow the manufacturer's directions, you can realize substantial savings.

*A well-ventilated boat shed and the materials for building a kayak: bolts of fiberglass cloth, a barrel of resin lying on its side, a hipbrace and seat-coaming mold suspended from a hook on the wall, and molds for the hull and deck (foreground). (*R.F.G.*)*

Health Warning About Resins

Resins are toxic and their effect is cumulative. Contact dermatitis—a skin rash—is a common complaint. Kidney and liver damage through prolonged inhalation of the fumes is more to be feared: the damage is irreversible and can be severe.

Therefore anyone working with resins—epoxy resin in particular—must ensure that there is plenty of moving air to dissipate the fumes. If working indoors, fans and face masks are essential.

ETHICS

Home-building often involves a problem of ethics. Few do-it-yourselfers are knowledgeable enough or have the time to create their own kayak design from scratch. The temptation to pull a mold off a race-winning boat can be strong, but such practice, in addition to being a possible patent violation, is just plain wrong. It is hard to imagine a group of people more often cheated than kayak manufacturers who promote the development of new designs.

PATCHING FRP

Minor breaks in the skin of a kayak are easily repaired with boat-building resins and the 6-ounce or 10-ounce fiberglass cloth generally available to the home builder.

Whether the patch is applied to the inside or outside is usually immaterial, though aesthetically the finished job will look a little neater if the patch is applied from the inside of the kayak. If the break is toward the bow or stern, however, the difficulty of working in the constricted portion of the interior will probably force you to use an outside patch. For a serious fracture you may want to patch both inside and out.

Sand the break and far enough around it to permit plenty of overlap for the patch. Sand thoroughly, right through to the cloth itself. You can speed the process with an electric disc-sander if the going is too slow.

The next step is to cut patches from the fiberglass cloth. Most patching requires two or more layers, so cut enough for the whole job beforehand. Remember to make patches large enough to cover the rupture with plenty of overlap.

You will need a small brush and a small hard-rubber roller to apply the resin. Mix the resin and hardener (or catalyst). Since a little goes a long way, a tin cup full of resin is usually sufficient for minor work. After you mix the resin there is no time for a coffee break—the resin will begin to set up in 20 minutes or so when the proper proportions are used. Spread some resin into the break, working it around the entire patch area. It's messy stuff, but you can use paper towels to catch the drips.

Next, put the patch in place (easier said than done—it slips around on the resin). With your roller, smooth out the air bubbles. If you don't get the bubbles out now, hard use will eventually lift the patch off. Repeat the process, applying another patch. You will need to apply three or four layers for a big break. Applying waxed paper to the kayak's exterior at the rupture will smooth the new resin. (The paper can be peeled off when the resin is set.) This is not essential but yields a neater result. Let the kayak sit overnight in a warm place. Seventy degrees Fahrenheit is a good temperature for curing resin.

Some manufacturers sell patch kits for their kayaks. Such a kit will produce better patches because the materials will be the same as those used in the original construction.

Emergency Repair

A few wraps of air-conditioner-duct tape will bandage a break adequately enough for emergency repair on the riverbank. So stash a roll of tape behind a flotation bag: it will come in handy some day.

THE BOAT FOR YOU

Nothing is more frustrating than buying something you really want and then discovering it is not quite right for you. To help you in buying a kayak or canoe here are a few things to consider.

Volume and Boat Type

If you weigh much over 150 pounds, forget about a low-volume boat, because with you in it, it won't have sufficient buoyancy to perform as the designer intended. If you are much under 120 pounds a high-volume boat won't be suitable, for despite your weight it will tend to sit on top of, rather than in, the water. However, if you plan to carry much duffle, a high-volume boat is almost mandatory.

The newcomer to kayaking should seriously consider a slalom-type boat. By their design, wildwater (downriver) kayaks are frustratingly tippy unless they are traveling at speed—remember the bicycle analogy—and for a while you can expect to spend as much time swimming as paddling. By contrast, the slalom boat is stable, and, thanks to its maneuverability, is a lot more fun to paddle.

Turn the slalom-type boat over. The V at the bow end of the hull is a good indicator of the type of performance you can expect. The longer the V and the more it is defined, the easier the straight-ahead paddling. If you contemplate much flatwater paddling this is a good choice. The less V and the more rounded the bow, the better the turning capability: this hull is best suited for strictly whitewater paddling because it allows fast turning.

Comfort

Comfort is a basic in choosing a recreational kayak. Racing kayaks are designed to get the job done, period, so their comfort is a secondary consideration.

If you are broad through the beam or amply padded be sure to sit in a kayak before you buy it. The fit should be acceptably snug so you won't slide around in the seat. Too much width can be remedied by taping foam padding to the hipbraces.

Be sure the footbraces will adjust to your needs. Some long-legged people simply can't find a comfortable position. Here again the fit should be comfortably snug. The knees should snuggle into the kneebraces. Seated in the kayak on the ground you should be able to wiggle the boat onto its side by rocking sideways. (Incidentally, during your first few times in your new kayak you may find a foot or leg going to sleep on you. Get on shore and try a little toe-touching to keep them awake; as your legs become used to this new position the condition usually goes away.)

Where to Look

Several U.S. manufacturers are licensed to fabricate boats from the molds of top designers. Currently most of these designers are Germans, since Germany is a hotbed of whitewater sport. At this writing the big names in whitewater design are Hahn, Lettmann, and Prijon of Germany and Mendesta of Belgium. However, there are sound American designers like Sedivec of California and Hauthaway in Massachusetts, to name only a couple.

Because kayaks consume a good deal of space in a showroom, retailers rarely have on display more than a couple of boats for comparison. Still, a good retailer will have manufacturers' catalogues showing a complete range of designs from European and North American designers.

Races provide a fine opportunity to see how the different boats perform. And maybe you'll pick up some free advice, because kayakers are a friendly lot and enjoy enlisting newcomers to their sport.

Secondhand Boats

There are good buys to be had in secondhand kayaks—if you can find them. Again, races are one place to look, since racers often bring with them an extra boat they want to sell. However, in addition to the preceding considerations, there are several things to keep in mind when you're looking at a used boat to buy.

First, since kayak design has come so far so fast, some older craft of early design will not perform to contemporary expectations. So try to verify the designer and model if possible.

Then, be particularly suspicious about evidence of repair. Minor patchwork is acceptable if the repair work is neatly done. Great expanses of patchwork—evidence that the boat has been crunched against a midstream boulder by the current—are worth a little more suspicion. In this case verify that this type of work has been done with the same materials used to construct the boat initially. The large patch should be structurally compatible with the rest of the craft.

3 *Paddles and Equipment*
[R . R . A .]

A SURE-FIRE WAY to recognize a kayak paddle even from a distance is that it has two blades. They dip into the water in a cycling motion, thus giving the kayaker a strokes-per-minute advantage over the canoe paddler.

Let's take a close-up look at the anatomy of a kayak paddle.

Its over-all length is about 7 feet, and it weighs from 2 to 3½ pounds. Circumference of the shaft is generally 4 inches, tapering from fully round at midpoint to elliptical near the throat, which is the region where each blade joins the shaft.

Types of Kayak Paddles

Most paddles look pretty much alike. Slalom racing paddles are more robust than recreational ones because of the extreme demands made by this particular competition.

Wildwater paddles usually have asymmetrical blades whose ends are slanted to permit a cleaner entry and withdrawal in the all-important Forward stroke. In addition, wildwater racers prefer paddles longer than the slalom type in order to gain a little more straight-ahead power.

The Blades

Each blade, whether symmetrical or not, has two edges and a tip (the end of the blade), and though blades vary in dimensions they

Kayak blades are "feathered"—set at right angles—and slightly curved for more power in stroking. (L.C.C.)

are usually about 8 inches wide and 18 inches from tip to throat.

Kayak blades have one constant design feature that makes them highly efficient: they are *feathered*, meaning that they are set on the ends of the shaft at a right angle to each other. This decreases wind resistance and deflection, for while one blade is pulled through the water, the other slices horizontally through the air.

Each blade has a power side—sometimes called the "face" or business side—which is the surface that pushes against the water, and a non-power side that is often referred to casually as the back. Most kayak blades are spooned: that is, they are slightly concave on the power side to get more purchase on the water during a Forward stroke (we use the same principle when we cup our hands as we swim the crawl).

Control

Kayak paddles, because the blades are feathered, have either right- or left-hand control. Control refers to the hand that maintains a constant grip on the shaft during the Forward stroke. The noncontrolling hand opens slightly while its blade is in the air to allow the shaft to rotate.

It doesn't make much difference whether you use a right- or left-hand-controlled paddle. Adapting to one or the other is quite easy—it's not like swinging a baseball bat where you are either a leftie or a rightie. It is easy to tell whether you are hefting a left- or right-hand-controlled paddle. Pick up the paddle in both hands. It is a right-hander if the power side of the right blade faces down and the power side of the left blade faces behind you. Vice versa, and it is a left-hander.

For the sake of simplicity, throughout this book we assume that the paddler is using a right-hand-controlled paddle.

MATERIALS AND CONSTRUCTION

The very best wooden paddles are aesthetic delights. It takes a master's touch, good glue, and exquisitely grained woods to fashion these lovely things.

Wooden paddles are built as separate halves that are fastened in the middle with a scarf joint. The blades are constructed of multiple laminations and are often faced with veneer; a metal or fiberglass cap protects the tip of the blade. The shaft is laminated with an ash core clad in spruce, with the ash extending into the blade for support.

There are many fiberglass-bladed paddles on the market. Blades are fabricated of fiberglass cloth and resin, sometimes curing in molds under high pressure at high temperatures. Shafts may be wood, aluminum, or fiberglass. The shaft inserts into the blades and, in the best paddles, extends deeply into the blades for strength.

CHOOSING A PADDLE

Price is a good but not totally trustworthy guide to quality. And quality is of prime importance, for if a blade snaps in the rapids you have a real problem.

A paddle must be rugged yet light and should balance well in your hands. Actual paddle weight is far less important than balance. If the bulk of a paddle's weight lies in the blades (a drawback usual

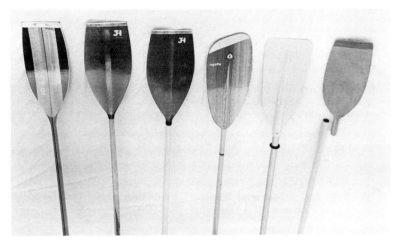

A sampling of kayak paddles includes (left to right): (A) an all-wood slalom paddle, (B) a fiberglass-blade, wood-shaft slalom paddle, (C) a fiberglass-blade, metal- or fiberglass-shaft slalom paddle, (D) an all-wood wildwater paddle, (E) a plastic-blade, metal-shaft slalom paddle, and (F) a kit paddle, which it put together with epoxy. (R.F.G.)

in inexpensive paddles), the paddle, despite an over-all light weight, will feel heavy in use.

Wooden paddles feel warm to the touch even in cold weather. But they have two disadvantages to consider: price, if you want a good one; and the periodic need to re-varnish. Inexpensive wooden paddles, typically constructed with blades nailed to the shaft, lack strength, and therefore their value in whitewater is questionable.

Gone are the drawbacks of price (although prices are rising) and maintenance if you opt for a fiberglass-bladed paddle. For recreational use this is a very good choice. This paddle will float, but if a blade should snap the broken piece will sink. Fiberglass-bladed paddles can be got from some manufacturers in kit form (you insert the shaft into the blades and epoxy them in place).

Take-apart paddles are excellent as spares. The two halves of the shaft are joined by interlocking metal sleeves, which fasten with a screw; the paddle can be put together to give either right- or left-hand control. The halves can be stored in your kayak or taped to the deck while you're running a river.

The following is a guide to suitable length for a kayak paddle.

Your Height	For Slalom	For Wildwater or Cruising
5′4″	80″	83″
5′6″	81″	84″
5′8″	82″	85″
5′10″	83″	86″
6′	84″	87″
6′2″	85″	88″

WHITEWATER CANOE PADDLES

The whitewater-canoe paddle—which has a single blade and is shorter than the kayaking type—differs little in method of construction or materials from the kayak paddles just discussed.

As for basic design, the whitewater-canoe paddle has a contoured T-shaped grip that allows the paddler to retain stout hold of his

A whitewater canoe paddle has a single, flat blade and a T-shaped hand grip. (L.C.C.)

paddle despite changing the pitch of the blade. Also, the blade is flat rather than spooned.

For C–1 racing and long-distance flatwater cruising, a relatively longer paddle (eyebrow-high when stood on end) is used. For C–2 racing and shallow rivers a shorter (chin-high) paddle is needed.

The standard solid spruce, ash, or maple paddle used by open canoeists is unsuitable for severe whitewater conditions. These paddles are heavy, often warp, and the blades may split in rocky waters.

Equipment

Whitewater kayaking is a safe sport for several reasons. For one, technique, honed by several decades of competition, makes it possible to have tight control while running the rapids. For another, the dynamics of fast-moving water have been thoroughly studied. Further, the modern fiberglass kayak is designed to be responsive in even the roughest of waters. And finally, whitewater kayaking has specialized equipment for the safety of the paddler and his kayak.

Safety lies in using all the equipment that a particular situation may require.

In the early 1960's most equipment for whitewater paddling was pretty makeshift—bicycle helmets to protect the head, innertubes used for flotation, homemade (and usually ill-fitting) spray-skirts. However, over the years modern technology has provided kayaking with excellent safety gear. This section discusses equipment for the paddler—lifejackets, helmets, wet-suits and other clothing; and for the kayak—spray-skirts and flotation bags.

Lifejackets

Mandatory: 1 October 1973—2. Boats less than sixteen (16) feet in length and all open canoes and kayaks: one Type I, II, III or IV PFD [Personal Flotation Device] **for each person on board.** From *Personal Flotation Devices: Requirements for Recreational Boats,* published by U. S. Department of Transportation, U. S. Coast Guard.

A Type I lifejacket is designed to turn its unconscious wearer face up in the water and has a minimum buoyancy of 22 pounds in the adult size. Type II is designed to do the same thing, but its buoyancy requirement is 15½ pounds. Type III is designed to keep a conscious person in a vertical or slightly backward position in the water and has the same buoyancy as a Type II jacket. Type IV PFD's are throwable—buoyancy cushions and ring buoys—and therefore are rescue devices not suitable for paddlers. All wearable PFD's produced since the rating system went into effect are so designated. If they were manufactured earlier, ask the dealer to show you the serial number, which can be equated to the rating system thus: Type I equivalents are Nos. 160,002 through 160,005; Type II numbers are 160,052 and 160,060; Type III's equivalent is No. 160,064.

This sounds mighty technical, but what it sugars-off to is adequate safeguards in case you get dumped in turbulent water and maybe are groggy to boot. So let's assume that all the lifejackets in the store are up to regulation: what other things are important to you as a whitewater boater?

What to Look For

A whitewater lifejacket should be light in weight; durable, so it will resist damage in tumbling rocky waters; close-fitting but comfortable; roomy in the armholes to permit free paddling action; and short enough to wear over your spray-skirt.

The vest-type life preservers with zipper or strap closure are preferred by most competitive paddlers. These vests are expensive, but they meet the basic requirements of comfort and generally provide a close fit that doesn't interfere with paddling. Although adequate for safety, the inexpensive, bulky, horse-collar variety are clumsy in and out of the water.

Flotation is achieved by several means: closed-cell foam, inflation, or kapok-filled vinyl sacks. In terms of durability the cell systems are preferable: a burst kapok-filled sack renders the whole life preserver useless, and it should be discarded.

The belt-type life preserver should not be chosen for paddling;

it will not support the head and shoulders, only the midriff. For the same reason the throwable Type IV's are useless—and they are noted for floating away in open-canoe upsets in whitewater. (Attached to a line, however, these same Type IV's are good back-ups at whitewater races, for they can be hurled by helpers from the river-bank.)

HELMETS

Any type of helmet is better than no helmet at all. Although water flowing around a rock will form a cushion, and upside down in a kayak you exert considerable drag, the time may come when a rock and your head collide.

When little else was available, bicycle-racing helmets were worn even though they provided only limited protection. Three or four padded leather ribs cover the top of the head and join to a hatband rib; cushioning is provided should a rib strike a rock. If the rock strikes between the ribs, however, there is no protection.

In contrast, rock-climbing helmets provide a hard outer shell,

Four styles of helmet include (left to right): a bicycle-racing helmet, a rock-climbing helmet, a hockey helmet, and—the best choice—a whitewater helmet. (R.F.G.)

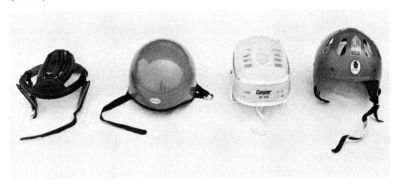

thick cushioning on the interior shell, and a snug, almost watertight fit. It is important when considering this type of helmet to be sure it provides sufficient protection for the fragile temple area. Because they are not adjustable, fit is important: try one on, and bend over with the chin strap unfastened: if the helmet slowly releases from your head, it's a good fit.

Hockey helmets provide good temple protection—and good drainage, which is important when executing the Eskimo Roll. The three-piece construction of the outer shell can be adjusted to your head size. The interior of the helmet is thinly padded.

Whitewater helmets are now imported to North America from Europe. They are light, with good drainage and an adjustable hatband. The outer shell is suspended above an inner webbing that fits over the skull.

WET-SUITS AND OTHER CLOTHING

Until the water temperature hits 50° Fahrenheit, wear a diver's wet-suit. In 36° F. water you could be immobilized in 10 minutes without one (in 40° F., 13 minutes; in 44°, 18 minutes; and in 48°, 25 minutes). A wet-suit makes an upset into cold water only a dunking, not an end to the day's boating, or even the beginning of a possible tragedy.

Wet-suits eliminate the need to carry extra clothes. You won't stay dry in a wet-suit, but you *will* stay warm and comfortable. In addition, they provide some protection from scrapes against underwater rocks should you go for an inadvertent swim.

Wet-suits come as jacket and pants, and in one piece like a jumpsuit. The legs and arms zip to provide a snug fit; the front of the suit zips from crotch to neck. In the two-piece suit, the jacket has an extended back flap that is drawn up through the crotch and attached at the front of the jacket. There is also a one-piece shorty model (often used by surfboarders) that has elbow-length sleeves and mid-thigh-length trouser legs. Some kayakers cut off the jacket sleeves above the elbows or at the arm holes for less restriction when paddling.

Thick wet-suit material constricts paddling action. In general,

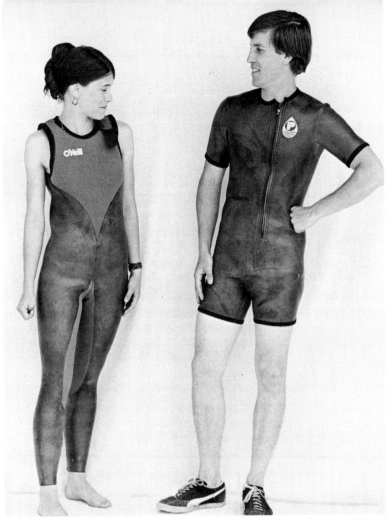

Left—a jumpsuit-style wet-suit; right—a shorty wet-suit. Both are made of neoprene. (R.F.G.)

³⁄₁₆-inch neoprene is a good thickness, being a compromise that allows both good insulation and yet some flexibility; ⅛-inch neoprene provides less insulation but more flexibility.

For Hands and Feet

Some kind of gloves for cold-weather paddling is essential because the cold wind quickly numbs wet fingers. Cotton or leather

The fist portion of a pogie slips onto the paddle shaft; the kayaker wears the wrist covering and attaches the parts with velcro fasteners. (L.C.C.)

work gloves are adequate. Wet-suit gloves are quite expensive, but they work well if not too bulky; leather driving gloves treated with a waterproof substance offer good protection without being bulky.

A fairly recent innovation to protect hands from chill and resulting cracked skin—while still allowing the all-important though subtle direct contact with paddle—is the "pogie" (pronounced po-ghee). Pogies are pieces of ⅛-inch neoprene that fit around each wrist like a sleeve and are cut in such a way that, as you grip your paddle with your bare hand, the neoprene can be wrapped around and under your fist and back over the top of your knuckles to rejoin itself at your wrist. Each pogie is held in place with a self-adherent nylon material that will pull away easily if you wish to remove your hand from the paddle-shaft; a well-designed pair of pogies will also let you slide your hands along the shaft. Some pogies are attached to the paddle-shaft, to be removed in warm weather and, if they have self-closures, installed again when paddling is chilly.

Wet-suit boots keep your feet delightfully warm, but they wear quickly if used for walking on shore. Best to buy a pair of cheap sneakers a couple of sizes too large and wear them over the wet-suit bootees. If you are not particular about toasty warm feet, just a pair of old sneakers or running shoes will do. Don't wear hiking or work boots because they will make swimming very difficult.

Paddling Jackets

In chilly weather a jacket is needed to protect the upper body from the cold spray, if the wet-suit is not needed or if it doesn't have full-length sleeves. Your lifejacket protects and insulates the trunk, so a paddling jacket's main purpose is to cover your arms and shoulders.

A lightweight, uninsulated nylon jacket or parka is ideal. When wet, it dries amazingly quickly and there is no restriction to your paddling, thanks to the fabric's lightness. Jackets with elasticized ribbing at the cuffs should be avoided because the ribbing holds the water, creating a cold, clammy band around your wrist.

FLOTATION FOR YOUR BOAT

Fiberglass doesn't float, so a flotation system is necessary to prevent your boat from filling with water and sinking after you make a Wet Exit. Flotation also keeps an overturned kayak riding high in the water, thus preventing serious damage from collisions with rocks if it is swept downstream.

Innertubes and inflatable beach balls originally were used. Their drawback is that, unless they are tied securely in place, they can work free in an upset and simply float out of the boat.

Far superior is the fitted flotation bag. These vinyl bags are

Fitted flotation bags (stern bag, top; bow bag, below) keep an overturned kayak riding high in the water, and they won't work loose in an upset. (R.F.G)

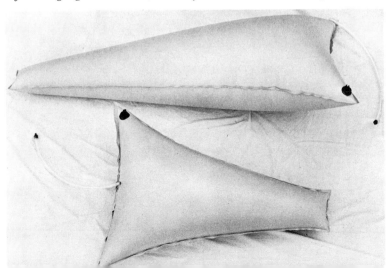

tapered to fit into the ends of the kayak. A small one is placed ahead of the footbraces, a larger one behind the cockpit. The typical bag has an oral inflation hose with a push-pull sealer similar to that in inflatable camping mattresses. Also, bags are equipped with large valves that can be opened to deflate the bag.

Some older bags are made with dual chambers: in the unlikely event that one chamber were to puncture, the other would still provide a measure of flotation.

SPRAY-SKIRTS: DESIGN AND MATERIALS

A spray-skirt is essential to keep whitewater from sloshing over the cockpit into the boat, and to keep the boat watertight while executing the Eskimo Roll. Used in flatwater, it keeps water from dripping off the paddle-shaft into your lap. And in cold weather a spray-skirt helps immeasurably to keep the lower part of your body snug and warm.

The spray-skirt is made with a full sleeve that covers your lower torso. The outer edge of the skirt is turned over to contain an elasticized cord. This outer edge is drawn over the coaming of the cockpit to produce a snug, drum-top fit.

Some spray-skirts are more watertight than others, but no spray-skirt should be so watertight that it cannot be released. All should have some form of a release-loop located at the forward point of

The elasticized edge of the spray-skirt fits snugly over the cockpit coaming. The release loop should always hang on the outside *of the spray-skirt.* (R.F.G.)

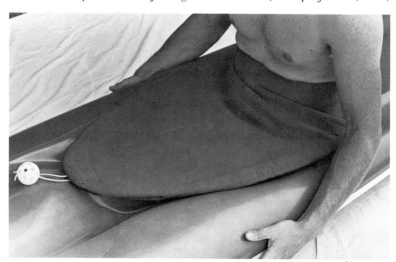

the skirt or along the side, should you decide to Wet Exit while upside down. A pull on this release-loop pops the spray-skirt off the coaming. *Never forget to expose the release-loop when attaching the skirt to the cockpit.*

NEOPRENE

The material used to make most wet-suits, neoprene, is supremely watertight and warm, and it wears well, as there is no waterproof coating to crack and flake off. A shock-cord is used for the coaming attachment. The sleeve around the waist is purposely cut small and depends on the material's natural elasticity for a snug fit.

Adjusting a neoprene spray-skirt to your size is accomplished by cutting away (or adding) material and re-glueing.

COATED NYLON

Skirts of this material release easily but, as the fit around the coaming is less snug than with neoprene, they can let some water into the kayak. Also, with extended use the coating will crack and flake off.

Drawstrings on the torso-sleeve and on the edge of the skirt are the means of attachment. Elasticized waistbands are normally provided.

PRICE GUIDE

The retail prices below were typical for 1974. However, much of the gear is manufactured from petroleum-based materials, so subsequent prices may be higher.

K–1:	$275 (kit $150)
C–1:	$325
C–2:	$400
Paddle:	$50–$60 (wood); $30–$40 (fiberglass)
Spray-skirt:	$18 (coated nylon); $25 (neoprene)
Flotation bags:	$15 a pair
Helmet:	$7 (hockey type); $18 (whitewater type)
Lifejacket (vest):	$25
Wet-suit:	$75 full length; $30 shorty

Take heart. If you are willing to do it yourself there are kits for wet-suits, life-vests, spray-skirts, paddles, and, of course, boats. In addition, if you join a club that has its own molds, materials, and workshop, you probably can build a boat for about $100.

4 *Basic Kayaking Technique*
[J . E .]

ONCE UPON A TIME Nathaniel Hawthorne remarked that his friend Henry Thoreau had told him it was necessary only to *will* a boat to go in any direction, and the boat would immediately assume the desired course as if imbued with the spirit of its pilot. Perhaps Thoreau was simply being a good salesman for the joys of boating on Walden Pond or the Concord River; certainly he wasn't talking about any craft that resembles the modern sporty kayak.

Applying basic technique in a tricky situation, this kayaker paddles confidently in a tidal rapids in the Atlantic Ocean. (J.T.U.)

Plan of Presentation

The purpose of this chapter is to nail down all the basic kayaking procedures. They will be constant points of reference throughout the rest of the book, and any variations in method can be superimposed for the special circumstances dealt with in later sections.

1. Throughout, it will be assumed that the paddler is a competent swimmer, and is ready to don sensible protective equipment after graduating from the shallow pool to deep and/or flowing water.

2. The sporty, ultra-maneuverable little slalom kayak will be the "demonstration model" for the steps that follow. This choice is partly because it is the favorite all-purpose boat for whitewater, and partly because it requires the widest range of paddling technique. Owing to hull design, the cruising or touring kayak is much easier to track, and the wildwater racing kayak is hard to turn at all as the result of emphasis on forward speed. Therefore if the newcomer to the sport learns how to control, stabilize and propel the tippy, mind-of-its-own slalom kayak, he or she can apply this acquired technique to managing the less recalcitrant boats.

3. Since every good paddler becomes virtually ambidextrous in the course of getting into the water and practicing, the matter of handedness and master-sidedness doesn't enter into basic kayaking techniques. So the procedures described hereafter will *start from the right*. Anyway, it will keep things neater for the beginning kayaker.

4. With the growing number of women kayakers, I wish someone would invent a suitable third-person-singular pronoun to denote a human being of either sex. Meanwhile, for simplicity's sake, *she/her/hers* can be read for the masculine pronoun. Kayaking is truly the whitewater sport for everybody.

My first kayak was named *Igluk* after the Eskimo god of mischief —and with good reason. One day during the early stages of my relationship with *Igluk* on a placid New Hampshire stream, a farmer haying close by noticed my predicament and called out: "You'll have to show 'er who's boss!"

So I was forced to learn kayaking technique. Which boils down to: (1) knowing how to get in and out of my boat; (2) knowing how to right myself when the kayak tips over; and (3) knowing how to paddle it so it will go precisely where I want it to go in any kind of water—in circles, sideways, forward and backward. And I found out how much my back, hips, abdomen and legs contribute to control and propulsion.

DRY RUN: ADJUSTMENTS

If you're new to kayaking you must first of all shed the notion that you sit in a kayak: what you really do is *wear* it, because the kayak feels almost like an extension of your body. Then, ideally, it will respond to a command from your brain.

There are a few things, though, that you'll need to check out before you wear your kayak in the water, because if the fittings are too tight your legs will soon fall asleep, and if the fittings are too loose you'll rattle around inside the boat like a loose tie-rod.

FOR LEGS, BACK AND KNEES

If you are a tall person you may wish to move the footbraces forward toward the bow to be sure there'll be enough room for your legs to stretch out.

Some kayaks come equipped with a back-strap that can afford a measure of support to your lower back. This strap, which is often made of canvas webbing or rubber about 2 to 3 inches wide, stretches between the hipbraces just behind the seat. It can be adjusted to give you the firmness you need in order to feel comfortable yet snug in the seat.

Carefully run your fingers over the inside surface of the kneebraces just forward of the seat under the coaming. This is to make sure that there are no rough spots that might irritate your knees when you press them tightly against the braces. Any roughness should be smoothed out.

Now the spray-skirt

Because its purpose is to keep all water out of the kayak so your lower body will remain warm and dry when you're paddling, your spray-skirt must fit you and your boat snugly—*but not too tightly*, lest it constrict your movements.

Step into the spray-skirt and draw it up to your waist. Cloth spray-skirts often have an adjustable drawstring, which is a handy feature. Neoprene spray-skirts seldom need adjustment at the waist since they are so flexible. But if necessary, the waist opening can be made smaller by cutting a 6-inch-long V out at the waist, and gluing the two sides back together with wet-suit cement (in sewing, this would be called "making a dart"). Or if the waist is too small, simply cut a 6-inch slit at the waist, into which a slender, pie-shaped wedge of neoprene can then be cemented, enlarging the waist to the desired fit.

Once the waist is adjusted you're ready to try the spray-skirt on the coaming. Still on dry land, step into the kayak—being sure to "hike up your skirt" on the backside before you lower yourself into the seat (if it is caught under your derrière it will be awkward to extricate after you're settled in the cockpit). Extend your legs forward until your feet touch the footbraces, and rest your knees against the kneebraces. If the seat and the foot-, hip- and knee-braces all fit properly, you'll begin to feel what it means to "wear a kayak."

Using both hands, tuck the skirt under the outside of the rolled edge of the coaming, *always starting from the rear* and working your way forward. Some skirts are supplied with a release-loop or some other safety device that releases the skirt immediately in case of emergency. If yours is, make sure the loop sticks out ready for use; then try it, to ensure that it will slip the spray-skirt off the coaming.

The spray-skirt should fit snugly enough around the coaming to be watertight. It should also have enough flexibility so it will slip off the coaming if you draw your knees up and push yourself up and away from the kayak. Try this a couple of times to satisfy yourself that the spray-skirt will come away from the coaming when necessary.

STEPPING IN/OUT WHEN IT'S AFLOAT

Once you've discovered what it is like to wear a kayak on dry land, your next move is to locate a quiet, shallow pond, lake or pool and learn how to enter a kayak while it is resting on the water.

Bobbing gently at the water's edge, your little craft with its rounded bottom and 23-inch width offers a tiny cockpit that seems hardly big enough to get into.

As you look down at it, your first inclination might be to place your foot somewhere in the middle of that cockpit.

Your next move might be to put some weight on that foot.

Your next—and final—move will be to hold your nose quickly as the kayak skitters away and you fall headfirst into the drink. (Don't laugh: this actually happened years ago in the most polluted section of the Potomac River to a first-time kayaker who eventually became national champion.)

Stepping in

Here's what you do instead. Place your kayak parallel to and against the bank or poolside in shallow water and, assuming that you are entering the kayak from the *right*, hold your paddle behind you with both hands. Squat down facing the bow. Reaching across the cockpit, hook the thumb of your left hand—which is still gripping the paddle-shaft—under the coaming behind the seat. Next, place the right paddle-blade so that it rests on the shore. Thus balanced by the paddle and crouched low next to the boat, step sideways into the boat, putting your left foot directly in front of the seat and slightly to the left of the centerline of the hull. Bring your right foot in next to the left foot, swing your fanny over the gunwale, and settle into the seat. Extend your legs forward until your feet touch the footbraces. Swing your paddle around in front of you, and you are ready for business.

Sometimes more experienced paddlers grip the coaming of the

Use your paddle as a brace to stabilize the kayak, and enter sideways, placing both feet in the cockpit before swinging your weight into the seat. (L.C.C.)

foredeck with their left thumb while holding the paddle in front of them (instead of holding the paddle and gripping the coaming behind them) as they enter, but this method is a little less stable, and therefore takes a little more practice.

STEPPING OUT

To get out of your boat, first make sure that your spray-skirt is free of the coaming—if you had it on. Then draw both knees up toward your chest. Place the paddle behind you and—while holding it—grip the rear of the coaming with your left hand just as you did while entering the kayak. Your right hand should grip the shaft, providing you with a measure of stability as the right paddle-blade rests along the shore. Carefully lift your right foot out of the boat and place it down on dry land next to the boat. Then do the same with your left foot and stand up.

You may want to practice your entry and exit several times to get them down pat before you try them with your spray-skirt on. And don't forget to hike up your skirt in the back before you lower yourself into the cockpit.

THE WET EXIT

As you begin to get the feel of what it's like to wear a kayak in the water, your first inclination may be to begin some Forward strokes to see how neatly the little craft will skim across the pond. This would be like undertaking to drive on an ice-slick road without knowing how to keep from slewing out of control: you had better know the technique for getting out of a skid even though you hope no emergency will require you to use it.

Similarly, with a kayak you should *learn first of all what to do if your boat decides to capsize*. This is one of those things that every paddler has in his repertoire, whether he's on a seemingly placid tour or is racing through whitewater on a slalom course. A good kayaker will rely on the Eskimo Roll, which will be described step-by-step a little later.

But first things first. So push away from the shore until you are in waist-deep water. Place your hands on the gunwales—you're chicken if you reach for the spray-skirt instead!—take a deep breath, then slowly capsize the kayak by leaning all the way over to your right.

Now you're upside down in the water, wearing a kayak. To prove that you don't feel uneasy about this new and unusual sensation, slowly slap the gunwales of the kayak three times before reaching for the coaming. Next, release your knees from the kneebraces and draw your feet up as you detach the skirt from the coaming. *All this should be done in slow motion.* Push the boat away gently with your feet as you slip out of the cockpit. If you are not wearing a mask or a nose-plug, exhale slowly through your nostrils to keep water out of your nose until you have surfaced.

Later, practice the Wet Exit with a paddle, keeping in mind not to let your paddle get away from the kayak: catch it immediately as you swim toward the bow or stern grabloop. You can hold the paddle *and* grabloop in one hand as you use the other hand to help propel yourself and your boat toward shore.

AND MAINTAIN CONTACT

Always maintain contact with your kayak.

The easiest way to do this is to keep one hand on the coaming as your head comes to the surface of the water, then swim quickly down to the bow or stern grabloop and begin to tow your boat to the nearest shore.

KEEP IT UPSIDE DOWN . . .

Always keep the kayak upside down when you're towing it after a Wet Exit: it will ride higher in the water that way, because of the air trapped inside.

AND STAY UPSTREAM YOURSELF

Always *stay upstream of your boat* when you're swimming with it in moving current, and you'll never be pinned on a rock or other obstruction.

If you keep this point in mind whenever you practice—even in the gentlest of currents—it can become an almost automatic reflex when you're obliged to exit in real whitewater.

SOLO KAYAK RECOVERY

Your companions have slipped around the bend of the river, just barely out of sight, and suddenly you capsize. Not yet knowing the Eskimo Roll you do a Wet Exit, remembering to keep your kayak upside down as you head for the nearest shore. You also remember to keep your paddle at hand.

But help may be out of earshot, and you are on your own.

Now what?

First, while you stand in shallow water, run the bow or stern of the kayak as far as possible up on the shore or poolside, *still keeping*

To empty the water from a capsized kayak, run the stern end up on shore or poolside while the boat is upside down, and lift the bow end to let water drain out of the cockpit. (L.C.C.)

the boat upside down. Slowly lift the lower end of the boat—the end that is lying in the water—and allow all the remaining water to slosh toward the cockpit and drain out.

Quickly snap the kayak over, float it, and Presto! you're ready to get in and catch up with your companions. And to remind them that kayaks should always stick together.

The Solo Kayak Recovery is also helpful when, more experienced, you are practicing maneuvers and so are tipping over rather frequently.

THE CRITICAL POINT

In learning to drive a car of course you have to get the hang of what the gearing, brakes and steering wheel do, before you head

Supporting yourself with an extended Paddle Brace, lean as far as possible to one side to determine the critical point of capsize—often an angle as great as 90 degrees. (L.C.C.)

out into rush-hour traffic. Likewise in kayaking, you must get used to your boat and its reactions—and its controls—before you point your bow toward open water and its currents.

We'll start with exploring the stability of your boat and determining the critical point of capsize.

The critical point is the maximum number of degrees you can lean to either side before you actually lose control and tip over. You'll be surprised at what an extreme angle it is.

To find your critical point, position your kayak close to land in about a foot of water and extend your paddle until the blade rests on the shore: you are now using the blade as a support when you lean too far. This support is a stabilizer, and it's a rudimentary form of the Paddle Brace—which will be mentioned soon under "Preliminary Exercises" to the Eskimo Roll, and will be discussed in full in "Stabilizing Strokes."

Now try first to lean at least 45 degrees without letting the boat slip out from under you. Then proceed to 90 degrees, where you wiggle back and forth with your hips just to show the kayak that you are in command. Recover, and repeat several times, on alternate sides, until you develop a good feel for the craft.

This exercise has an added importance because it gives you a sense of hip action and the power that the muscles of your abdomen and legs can exert on the kayak to make it react properly under you. This controlling action is the *hip-snap*, and it is one of the most important components of kayaking.

THREE BASIC CONTROL STROKES

The Sweep

The Sweep is a turning stroke.

(By the way, it is too early to go into the fine points of paddle-handling right now. This will be discussed in the section dealing with the Forward stroke. For now it is enough simply to hold your paddle comfortably with both hands, keeping in mind that the scooped side—or face—is the business side of the paddle-blade 99 percent of the time.)

Try a Sweep by placing the right blade in the water near the bow—at the 1 o'clock point—about 5 inches deep, then sweep out and around as far as you can without letting the blade sink deeper below the surface. In a slalom kayak one should be able to complete a round-the-clock turn in just three strong strokes.

Practice the Sweep both to the right and to the left.

The Draw

The purpose of the Draw stroke is to pull the kayak sideways in the water. And what a great move this is to have in your bag of tricks when you're running the rapids and a rock suddenly looms in front of you!

A

To turn using a Sweep stroke, bring the paddle around from 1 o'clock to 5 o'clock without letting the blade sink completely below the water's surface. (R.F.G.)

B

C

The Draw stroke moves the kayak sideways. Insert the paddle as far as the throat on the side toward which you want to move, and pull steadily toward you. Lean toward the paddle to increase leverage. (R.F.G.)

To perform the Draw, lean and reach out with the paddle to 3 o'clock. Lower the blade into the water as far as the throat, then pull the paddle steadily and evenly toward you, leaning strongly sideways toward the paddle to increase leverage and power. Remove the blade from the water as it approaches the gunwale.

It is also possible to draw while using your hips to hold the kayak on an absolutely even keel; that is, without leaning in the direction of the paddle.

Or, as an exercise to increase hip control, try holding a lean *away* from the direction of your paddle. You'll be surprised how easily the water slips under your kayak this way.

Practice drawing on either side for 50 yards at a stretch. At the Ledyard Canoe Club we sometimes held Draw-stroke races from one side of the pool to the other. Relay races can also be held in this manner.

The Scull

Sometimes it is important to maintain a lean longer than a normal Draw allows. This is where the Scull stroke comes in.

Actually, the Scull is not much more than a multiple Draw stroke wherein the blade never leaves the water. It cuts a slight arc through the water as it is pulled toward the gunwale, then slices its way out again away from the boat in a motion rather like forming a

The Scull stroke enables you to maintain a lean or maneuver your kayak sideways. Move the paddle in a slow figure 8 from bow to stern. (R.F.G.)

figure 8. It is a graceful maneuver, and a very nice way of moving your kayak into a better position laterally.

After a long hard paddle on a hot day, a good sculler can refresh himself by leaning far enough over while sculling to duck his head in the water (and even drinking the stuff if it isn't polluted).

Practice sculling on both the right and left sides for 50-yard intervals.

PREPARING FOR THE ESKIMO ROLL

A complete capsize followed by a self-recovery full-circle to an upright position is called the Eskimo Roll, and is probably the most famous maneuver in kayaking. There are people who can perform the full Eskimo Roll without using a paddle at all: of these, some can bring themselves back upright with only one bare hand; and a real stunt man can do it with only his clenched fist.

Formerly, the Roll was considered an advanced trick reserved for the expert. This attitude has undergone a change, though, and today the Eskimo Roll is regarded as so essential to safety that the beginning kayaker must master it *before* he ventures out on a river or lake.

Mastery of the Eskimo Roll not only assures an excellent margin of safety in most situations, but it also promotes psychological confidence and prepares the beginner for learning the other basics of handling a kayak. So what if you capsize? With a reliable Roll you can come back up immediately, ready for anything.

In trying to teach the Eskimo Roll to new kayakers I have been both an astonishing success and a miserable failure: some people catch on to the idea faster than I can demonstrate, while others flop around for months bewildered by the mystery of it all. There must be a direct relationship between a person's muscular co-ordination and the time it will take him to do a Roll quickly and confidently, for the well-co-ordinated kayaker can learn it in a very short time even with poor instruction, while someone with less physical harmony will simply have to be more patient. But the Roll, truly mastered, is like riding a bicycle: you never forget how to do it.

A person with only average co-ordination, therefore, should not be disheartened. One national champion I know of took an entire month to learn how to roll.

The following sequence for the Roll has evolved over the years, and is designed specifically for the average person who has no special athletic ability.

First—Observe

If possible, watch an expert perform the Roll several times in slow motion. Stand in shallow water, and with each of his revolutions concentrate your attention on a different aspect of the maneuver: notice where and how he grips his paddle; note the sweeping motion of his arms, then the motion of his upper body; pay particular attention to the blade angle. Study him in action from the front, from both sides, from the rear. Next, take a pair of goggles and watch his Roll from several underwater positions.

As you watch from all angles, this is what you see: A deliberate full capsize until he is completely upside down in the water; the placing of the paddle in the correct position and then the arc of his stroke sideways just under the surface; a hip-snap—and he's brought himself upright again, on the side opposite from the one he went down on.

Preliminary Exercises

Now that you have the over-all picture in mind, you're ready to get in your boat and perform in sequence the following exercises that build up to your own Eskimo Roll.

> *Note:* All the procedures described are accomplished in water *no more than 3 feet deep*—which will give ample clearance for even a tall person upside down in a kayak. The photographs to demonstrate the sequences were taken of paddlers in the shallow end of a regulation swimming pool, but the kayakers could just as easily have been practicing at the shallow edge of a pond if they had established that there were no obstructions underwater. (Of course in open or unfamiliar water each would have been wearing a helmet, as every capable boater does. Expertise is judged by control of one's boat, *not* by sloppiness about equipment.)

No. 1: THE ESKIMO RESCUE

This first exercise starts with a partial capsize and recovery back up on the same side, and it is designed to give the new kayaker confidence in his ability to control his boat and himself, and to demonstrate the value of the hip-snap in his recovery to an upright position.

Aside from your own boat, the only thing you need for the Eskimo Rescue is another kayaker stationed at 3 o'clock with the bow of his boat pointing directly at you and only a foot or so away from your right elbow.

Reach over and grab his bow with both hands, and slowly lower yourself to your right into the water, allowing your kayak to capsize while you maintain your grip on the bow of the helping boat.

Then, still hanging on to his bow, use a hip-snap to see if you can get your kayak back upright again without having to chin yourself too much on the rescue boat. Exerting pressure on your kneebraces will help your hip-snap immensely, so here you press your right

In the Eskimo Rescue, first allow your boat to capsize while you hold on to the bow of a friend's boat, which is positioned perpendicular to yours. To right yourself, combine hip-snap with a minimal pull on the rescue boat. (L.C.C.)

knee strongly in against its brace to add power to your hip-snap and force your kayak to slide back under you again.

The idea of this exercise is to rely chiefly on the hip-snap, and to use your arms and hands only to a minimum extent as you pull yourself upright.

Repeat, alternating the side you capsize on, until the procedure of recovery becomes second nature. And increase your lean as you practice, so you can go over with confidence the full 180 degrees, until you and your kayak are completely upside down, before you come back up with the help of the other boat.

Now you're ready to go all the way over *without using the stand-by craft to help you tip over.*

Bend forward at the waist—any capsize is smoother if your trunk is positioned low—lean to the right, and ease yourself into the water as your hands rest lightly on the gunwales.

Pause there upside down for a moment to let things settle. Then slap your hands on your hull as it lies above water to draw your partner's attention. He will quickly bring his boat over to you until his bow nudges your near hand. Grab his bow with both hands, give a good hip-snap to do most of the work, and bring yourself back up again.

The Eskimo Rescue sure beats having to wet-exit, to tow your boat to shore, and to bail it out before you can get going again. And the Rescue is particularly useful when a bunch of beginners are together practicing, or are training in an indoor pool.

No. 2: Assisted recovery to the opposite side

This exercise is similar to what you did in the Eskimo Rescue, except that here you make a 360-degree turnover, coming up on the *opposite* side in your recovery. You're getting closer to the actual Eskimo Roll, even though you rely on a helper to recover.

In Exercise No. 1 you got the hang of a controlled capsize to the right without assistance. Now, though, you will use the same method but you will *capsize to your left*. And the important part will be how you recover on the second half of the revolution—through the remaining 180 degrees—and come up on the right as before.

This kayaker, practicing an assisted recovery to the opposite side, had capsized to his left side and is recovering on his right side, using a friend's paddle to help pull himself upright. His head and shoulders should emerge last. (L.C.C.)

First, have a helper stand in waist-deep water on your right side just behind your cockpit. There he will position your paddle steadily on the surface of the water parallel to your boat and about 6 inches away from it.

Then, when he is ready, you will capsize to your left.

After you complete the capsize, reach across your body until you grasp the paddle-shaft that is being held for you (your helper must maintain firm control of the paddle, keeping it immovable).

Finally, pull yourself up toward the paddle and, at the same time, use your hips to make the kayak slide under you until you are completely upright again. However, *your head and shoulders must emerge from the water after the kayak has begun to assume an upright position.*

Try capsizing several times on either side until the recovery becomes a very natural and relaxed motion—and always with your head and shoulders coming up *last,* for this point is highly important to a successful Eskimo Roll. If you let your head and shoulders emerge first, your assistant can remind you by rapping his knuckles on your unsuspecting head as it comes up. A couple of sharp raps and you'll remember to keep your head down.

No. 3: THE LITTLE-FINGERS EXERCISE

The necessity of a good hip-snap in executing the Roll is the point of this one.

Ask a helper to stand in waist-deep water next to your cockpit facing you. Interlock the little finger of your left hand with the little finger of his right hand; interlock the little finger of your right hand with the little finger of his left.

Now gently capsize toward him, keeping your fingers interlocked with his. No fair grabbing his whole hand!

You are now upside down but still connected to your helper.

You will need herculean strength if you attempt to right yourself solely by pulling with your fingers in order to get your head and shoulders above water. Instead, exert pressure on your hip- and kneebraces in an effort to force the kayak to slide under you. You'll be surprised how easily the kayak does this, and how quickly you see daylight. The more hip and knee pressure, the less effort will be needed with your fingers.

And don't forget to practice the Little-Fingers Exercise capsized to the other side.

No. 4: THE PADDLE-BRACE RECOVERY

By now you are at ease in the controlled capsize, and you can employ good hip-snap to help get yourself topside again. Therefore with this exercise you are advancing to the self-recovery aspect of the Eskimo Roll: here you will begin to *paddle yourself upright.*

You have come far since you used a dry-land Paddle Brace in discovering your critical point of capsize when you were getting used to wearing a kayak. This time, though, it will be a real Brace, which uses leverage on the water instead of on solid ground.

But before you start, let's take a look at your paddle again to see how it will function in this maneuver.

Your Blade Angle in the Brace

The blades at each end of your kayak paddle are feathered, which means that they are set at a right angle to each other. Thus when one blade is flat on the water the other blade is standing up like a fin.

In addition, the chances are 10–to–1 that the blades are scooped—i.e., they have a slightly concave face, or business side, and a slightly rounded back. This spooned design makes your pull through the water more effective. However, it also means that your blade can "dive" when you swing it flat along the surface of the water in a Paddle Brace unless you *keep the leading edge slightly raised.*

Non-scooped blades will dive too, of course, if their leading edge is not slightly raised during a Brace.

Get set in water no more than 3 feet deep, and have an assistant close by to effect an Eskimo Rescue if your efforts get a bit scrambled before you get the knack of this new maneuver.

Lean to the right almost to the critical point of capsize. Next—still leaning—slap the face of your right-hand paddle-blade *flat on the surface of the water* near your bow at 1 o'clock. Then swing your blade—still holding it flat on the water—in an arc until it's about at 3 o'clock, and you will automatically resume an upright position.

Now lean a little farther, and right yourself with your Paddle Brace as before. Repeat, leaning more each time, until you can go well *beyond* the critical point, each time swinging the blade around to 3 o'clock in order to recover.

Eventually you'll be able to brace for several seconds while your shoulder and even part of your head are in the water, *and still recover*. At the end of your swing you may want to draw or scull a little to assist your recovery.

The Paddle-Brace Recovery should be practiced many times on both sides. And it is a good general warm-up exercise when you first get into your kayak before attempting rapids.

No. 5: The Half-roll to the right

This Half-roll contains the key maneuver for self-recovery in any Eskimo Roll, and it is the final exercise before you proceed to the full Roll itself.

The Half-roll is a controlled 180-degree capsize and recovery back up on the same side by initiating a Paddle Brace while you're upside down in the water, and by using "body English" mainly in the form of a strong hip-snap.

A kayaker prepares for a Half-roll to the right. Note the correct hand and paddle positions along the left gunwale. (L.C.C.)

You will recover without help from anybody else—but do have someone standing by in the water to assist you the first few times in case you can use a helping hand. And it would be a good idea to wear goggles or a face-mask: you'll welcome a clear underwater view of the pitch of your paddle-blade until you can bring off the recovery by feel alone.

Throughout the maneuver you will be using an *extended-paddle grip*—which increases the effective radius of your paddle, as you will see—and you *must maintain your blade angle by keeping its leading edge slightly raised.*

So start by holding your paddle alongside the left gunwale with your right hand somewhere comfortably near the middle of the shaft, palm down and thumb toward you. (This is where the "extended" part comes in: with your hand moved back on the shaft instead of its normal grip nearer the forward blade, you're adding about 18 inches to your paddle's range.)

Lay your forward blade flat on the water near your bow, *face up* (so it will be business-side *down* when you get completely capsized), and with its leading edge slightly raised. To maintain it at the correct angle and increase its leverage, reach your left hand back and, thumb down, grasp the tip of the rear blade to ensure that it stands up like a fin and thus maintains your forward blade approximately flat.

With your paddle set, bend forward for a smooth capsize and turn completely over to your right.

Upside down in the water, keep your paddle close to your left gunwale and at the surface of the water in the same position it was before you capsized. You're now ready to use the pressure of a Paddle Brace to initiate your recovery.

Swing the forward blade in a quarter-circle away from your bow, watching your leading edge through your goggles to ensure that it is slightly raised and thus will skim along the surface without diving. As you bring your blade around from your bow, give a good hip-snap to help get yourself upright again. Remember that the more pressure you exert against your right kneebrace, the more effective your hip-snap will be, and the more readily your kayak will slide under you as you come back up again.

If you can recover successfully on your very first try at the Half-roll you're some kind of athlete!

The rest of us, though, can probably use a little outside assistance. Thus:

1. Station a helper so he will be standing near the tip of your forward blade after you have capsized to the right.

Go completely over, and allow your friend to guide your blade lightly in the proper arc on the surface of the water. Immediately, you will feel the torsion produced by your upside-down Paddle Brace; at the same time you'll sense the effectiveness of the pressure exerted by your right knee in aiding the hip-snap portion of your recovery.

2. Move your helper to a position just behind your cockpit on

After capsizing in a Half-roll to the right, have a friend guide your blade in a Paddle-Brace arc on the surface of the water. This pressure, plus the force of a hip-snap, brings you upright. (L.C.C.)

For extra help in the Half-roll, have your helper move behind the cockpit and gently pull on the kayak to help you roll back up. (L.C.C.)

your left. When you capsize to the right, he will reach across the bottom of your hull, take hold of your left gunwale, and gently pull it back up as you work with paddle and hip-snap to get yourself upright again.

As you become more proficient, he will help less and less—until, at some point unknown to you, you are accomplishing your recovery without any help from him at all.

3. In the course of your practice with a helper you will get so accustomed to the feel of the correct angle of your forward blade that you no longer need the extra control derived from holding your rear blade by its tip. At this stage you may wish to move your left hand up to the throat of the rear blade and control the pitch of your forward blade from there.

No. 5½: Half-roll to the left

In many cases, people learning to roll will wish to continue working on one side until their Roll is perfected. However, the "compleat kayaker" is one who eventually masters the Eskimo Roll on *both* sides, and thus can recover from a capsize at will, righting himself from either side as it suits his fancy at the moment.

Therefore those paddlers whose goal is to be ambidextrous in the water will want to take some time out to practice the Half-roll to the left. The procedure is simply a reversal of the exercise used for the Half-roll to the right.

With your left hand at mid shaft and your right hand behind you holding the tip of your rear blade, place your forward blade on the water face up, just to the right of your bow and with its leading edge slightly raised. Capsize to the left and, when you're 180 degrees upside down, arc your forward blade back from the bow, give a strong hip-snap with good pressure on your left kneebrace, and recover to an upright position.

Repeat the maneuver with the aid of a helper until you have it down pat, and can recover confidently on your own.

Master-sidedness may be a slight factor here. Occasionally a paddler who has cinched his self-recovery on one side will take longer to perform the exercise well on the opposite side. The answer of course is to practice Half-rolls until there are no hang-ups with recovery on either side.

THE FULL ESKIMO ROLL

When you have nailed down the Half-roll and recovery, it is a simple matter to complete the full 360-degree Eskimo Roll.

You merely capsize to the opposite side from the one on which you initiated the Half-roll, and, when you're in position to start your self-recovery, you execute exactly the same paddle movement and hip-snap that brought you up from the Half-roll.

Thus if you're going to recover on your right, you place your paddle on your left and capsize to your left.

If you're going to recover on your left, then position your paddle correctly on your right and capsize to your right.

On the first couple of tries you may want a helper standing by as he did for the Half-roll practices—but he'll be there mainly for moral support. Actually, you are likely to find the full 360-degree

The complete sequence of steps in the
Eskimo Roll takes you full-circle from
the initial upright position (top of drawing) through the capsize and recovery.
(W.R.)

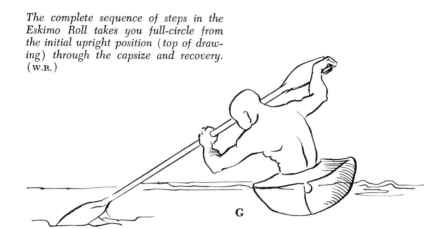

G

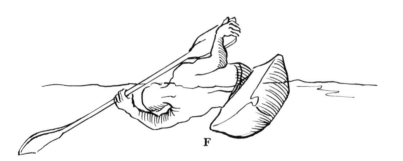

F

E

A

B

C

D

Roll easier, because you have momentum going for you as you reach the 180-degree mark in your capsize.

And remember: *How you capsize is far less important than WHAT YOU DO ONCE YOU'RE UPSIDE DOWN to get yourself topside to daylight again.*

SUMMING UP OTHER KEY POINTS IN THE ESKIMO ROLL

1. Hold your paddle in an extended grip and have the forward blade positioned perfectly, then capsize.

2. Keeping the leading edge of your forward blade slightly raised —lest it dive when you swing it around in the Brace movement— bring your blade flat in an arc from bow to side.

3. Exert pressure against your recovery-side kneebrace to give added strength to your hip-snap.

4. Synchronize your Brace and hip-snap so your boat slides under you *before* your shoulders and head emerge from the water.

THE ESKIMO ROLL IN CURRENT

Every newcomer to the sport who has gained confidence in the Roll as the result of honing his technique in pool or pond will be doubly pleased with the maneuver when it is executed with a gentle assist from flowing water.

Therefore the next step is to find a safe place in a river. "Safe" means a spot that is near the bank, is about 3 feet deep, has been thoroughly checked to be free of underwater obstructions, and has a modest current.

Which bank you choose to take off from is up to you: you are going to capsize in the current while leaning *upstream,* and recover on the *downstream* side. Therefore do your very first "river-reading" to decide how you will point your boat upstream initially to get broadside to the current.

Are you more comfortable in a recovery to the right? Then plan to have your left side upstream. If you're more proficient at recovering on the left, plan to get in position with your right side upstream.

Then put on your helmet and lifejacket and have a helper in the water standing by (these are rudimentary safety measures that show you have common water sense), paddle your kayak a few strokes to the chosen place—and try your Roll.

You will be pleasantly surprised at how much easier it is to roll as the current gives you added momentum.

When you feel completely confident about handling the Roll from an upstream capsize, practice rolling from a variety of positions in the river. You might even try recovering on the upstream side: it really isn't all that difficult.

. . . Then the "wild" Roll

Before you tackle the Roll in actual rapids, simulate whitewater conditions by sprinting for at least 20 yards in relatively flat water, then capsize suddenly without taking time to set your paddle-angle or otherwise position yourself correctly before you go over. Once underwater in a full capsize, get organized for a correct recovery—and roll back up.

Practice capsizing at full speed on both sides, with correct recovery. Be sure to sprint long enough so you're slightly out of breath—as you would be if paddling hard in demanding whitewater. And as you gain confidence, capsize while holding your paddle with only one hand.

. . . And finally in whitewater

Later, when you have truly learned to "read the river," will come the ultimate phase of this maneuver: the Eskimo Roll in whitewater.

When practicing your Roll in rapids it is more important than ever before to make sure the water is deep enough—the usual 3 feet is plenty—and that there is a quiet pool or "catch basin" just below your practice spot to give you a welcome parking place. Again you'll be surprised how easy the Eskimo Roll is.

And what a feeling of confidence it gives you! If in the future the rapids get sassy and pitch you around a bit, even tossing you over—so what? Simply roll back up and continue on your way. You may not have mastered the river, but you have mastered yourself.

The broken-paddle Roll

Most of today's paddles are strong enough to withstand all but the worst treatment, but there's still the chance that a blade will get wedged between submerged rocks and break—possibly causing a capsize as well. So a simple exercise like the following is worth the time spent in practice: it could come in handy some day.

First, get a paddle that has one blade broken and thus is useless as a lever for performing the Eskimo Roll. This shouldn't be a problem, because paddles break—when they do break—either at the throat or somewhere on the blade itself.

Second, pretend you don't know your paddle is broken, then capsize in the first stage of the Roll, and try to recover with the broken end. You'll feel immediately, as you swing the paddle around in its accustomed arc, that you are getting little or no leverage.

Third, slip back again into a fully capsized position, and simply *switch your paddle around in your hands* so you're now working with the good blade. Carefully set its angle with the leading edge slightly raised, sweep it out and around, using good hip-snap, and you will roll back up with the good half of the paddle.

THE DRIVING STROKES

Having got the Wet Exit and the Eskimo Roll under our belts, we can now concentrate on getting from here to there in a kayak. Let's start with the Forward stroke, examining its components and seeing how the paddle will work in our hands.

The Forward Stroke

The Forward stroke can be one of the most beautiful movements in all sport, exhilarating for the spectator and paddler alike. Knowledge and many hours of practice are required to perfect it.

In flatwater kayak racing an efficient and powerful Forward stroke is absolutely vital to success.

In whitewater races a smooth-flowing Forward stroke properly executed does wonders toward positioning the boater properly as he negotiates the gates.

And, lastly, a quiet day's cruise across a lake or down a stream for several miles is done in a greater degree of comfort, with less fatigue, if a good, efficient Forward stroke is learned beforehand.

How it works

Basically the Forward stroke is a cycling movement of arms and shoulders. It is similar in principle to pedaling a bicycle, and it must be executed with great precision and smoothness in order to be efficient. It is the economic application of effort properly done that permits the paddler to attain a greater sustained speed at less expenditure of energy.

Such a prolonged effort can be maintained only if the muscles relax in the course of the stroke. Fortunately, in kayaking the business of alternating your arms between the dip and the recovery will ensure this relaxation.

Body position

As you settle into your kayak, maintain a naturally comfortable position with your feet firmly against the footbraces and knees against the kneebraces. Now lean forward slightly—but not too far. And don't slouch: keep your head up and look forward.

With both hands palms down grasp the paddle in front of you so that it is parallel to the water level. Your hands should be about 3 feet apart and approximately 8 inches up the paddle-shaft from the throat. This position will make your arms create an angle of about 90 degrees at the elbows.

How the paddle will turn

Virtually all kayak paddles today are feathered, and the majority of these are spooned in such a way as to require right control or left control—with right-control paddles being by far the most common.

Therefore as you make a stroke on the right side with a right-control paddle, you will rotate the shaft a quarter-turn with your right hand so the blade will enter the water in the correct position. Simultaneously, your left hand relaxes a bit to allow the shaft to rotate.

To stroke on your left side, again rotate the shaft with your right hand so the left blade will enter the water properly, and then grip the shaft firmly with your left hand as you pull the left blade through the water.

A

B

C

The Forward stroke is basically a cycling motion of your arms and shoulders. The feathered kayak paddle is rotated during the stroke so that each blade enters the water in the correct position. The stroke includes three steps: the dip on the right side (A), the draw back to the midpoint of the kayak (B), and the recovery of the blade from the water (C). The paddle is then set to begin the same sequence on the left side (D, E, F). (R.F.G.)

D

E

F

The turning of the shaft with each individual stroke makes certain that the other blade just removed from the water will slice neatly through the air, offering little or no wind resistance.

If you find that your paddle is left-control (as we say earlier, this is determined by the spoon of each blade), then your left hand always turns the shaft while your right hand relaxes.

Components of the Forward stroke

We can divide the Forward stroke into three closely interrelated parts—the dip, the draw back through the water, and the withdraw/recovery.

1.   *The dip.* Lean slightly forward—but not too far. Extend your right arm forward as far as you can toward the bow and insert the right blade completely in the water. Meanwhile your left wrist should be at ear level, your left elbow pointed down and slightly away from the kayak to provide maximum leverage. The fingers of your left hand may be fairly relaxed on the shaft at this point.

2.   *The draw.* With full muscular effort, draw the blade straight back to the midpoint of the kayak *but not beyond.* Your right wrist is straight, but your right elbow flexes as the blade comes directly back alongside the kayak. To utilize more power, don't hesitate to turn your body and shoulders a little to the right as you draw the blade back. Put your body into the stroke, because if you let your arms do all the work, they'll soon tire.

While your right hand was dipping and drawing back, your left hand (which controlled the other half of the paddle) pressed straight forward toward the center line of the kayak at eye level. This movement of the left arm and hand is not unlike putting the shot in track, or delivering a straight left to the jaw of your opponent in boxing.

Don't allow the dip-and-draw arm to do all the work in each cycle of strokes: if you paddle this way you'll soon be fatigued (maybe after only a quarter-mile of paddling). Instead, think of the power of the Forward stroke as coming from two distinct sources: about 65 percent from your dip and draw, and about 35 percent from your forward punch with the other hand—while rhythmically moving your body and shoulders at the waist to the right and left to complement both draw and push. Both power sources working in harmony together not only produce an amazingly efficient Forward stroke with which you can paddle for miles, but they also create a graceful movement that is completely satisfying aesthetically.

3. *Withdraw/recovery.* Your right hand smoothly lifts the paddle from the water in a natural upward movement after the right blade passes the cockpit. Your left hand is now in a position to begin the dip of the left blade near the bow of your kayak to complete the stroke cycle.

BREATHING

Even when you're in pretty good physical condition, if you're a beginning kayaker you may suddenly find yourself out of breath after a fast spurt of Forward strokes. Why? Simple: maybe you forgot to breathe!

You've been careful to keep your head up to give those air passages to your lungs a chance to work for you. Now try taking one full breath for each right-left cycle of strokes. Faster breathing will rarely permit a full exchange of used air, but a steady and rhythmic movement of the lungs contributes to proper circulation and helps to prevent an oxygen deficiency. A good rule to remember is: *INHALE as your right hand dips, EXHALE as your left hand dips.*

Paddling on a full stomach impairs your breathing. Not to mention ruining your digestion.

Don't talk unnecessarily while paddling: it disturbs the rhythm of your breathing.

And remember to keep your head up at all times, although you're leaning forward for added power.

KEEPING ON TRACK

Proper tracking—keeping a kayak running in a straight line—requires a subtlety of paddle-angle and delicate paddle-pressure that come only from experience. What this boils down to is making tiny corrections with each paddle stroke in order to keep the boat going straight, rather than employing one or two big forceful corrections on each side after the kayak has begun to turn off course.

Now that you have your kayak moving along in one direction by using the Forward stroke, don't leave it at that. Keep paddling for a mile or more each day until you begin to feel your two power sources working together smoothly. Don't be discouraged—it will take time. Don't be alarmed if your little craft occasionally acts like a spooked horse and veers off in some unlikely direction quite different from where you wish to go. Your kayak is merely displaying a "tracking syndrome." However, with a few miles of paddling under your keel your little kayak will recognize you as master and begin to behave.

BALANCING EXERCISES

Give yourself a change in practicing your Forward strokes by leaning to the right with each dip to the right, and leaning to the left with each left dip. Lean far enough with each stroke so your gunwale is awash.

Practice leaning for a hundred yards at a stretch without losing your rhythm. On a long paddle across a lake this can help break up the monotony a bit.

When you're proficient at maintaining rhythm while leaning on your dip side, lean on the side opposite from each stroke for a hundred yards at a clip. This is a great exercise for loosening up your hips and for practicing general boat control and stability.

The Back Stroke

Normally you'll want to use Forward strokes to get you where you want to go. But occasionally you'll find yourself in a situation where a good, hard Back stroke can help you get in a desired position. (You'll also use this stroke in Backferrying—which we'll get to when we start to practice in a current.)

Lean back a little, instead of bending forward at the waist. Without changing the basic Forward stroke position of the spooned side of the blade, dip your right paddle into the water slightly behind you. The back of the blade is now your "business side" as you *push* it forward in the water, using a lot of body pressure. Meanwhile your left hand is *pulling* the left blade back in the air.

Follow the same procedure on the other side if you need to take more than one Back stroke to get yourself positioned advantageously.

A

For the Back stroke, dip the paddle into the water behind you (A), then push it forward through the water (B). (R.F.G.)

B

Even though you'll seldom need to keep back-stroking, it's worthwhile to practice the cycle: then you'll have the skill to bring off a strong, precise Back stroke when you want it.

The dip and push of each Back stroke form a perfectly natural and easy motion, and are a cinch to learn. But after you think you're pretty good at it, try leaning toward your stroking side; then try leaning away from each Back stroke.

If you are honest about leaning, some interesting things can happen—including a capsize. But as a kayaker you don't mind getting wet. And it offers a chance to practice your Eskimo Roll.

Ferrying

The Ferry is a controlled sideslip across a current, whereby the paddler uses the power of the water against his partially angled kayak to carry his boat where he wants it to go—instead of pointing his bow directly toward his objective and stepping on the gas. It is at its most effective in whitewater, where the strong swirl of water can be the initial propellant, aiding the boater to go crabwise across the current.

We've not yet graduated fully to whitewater, however, so the beginner must settle for a stream that has moving current and is clear of obstacles in which to practice Ferrying. There he can learn how the forces of paddle, current and weight distribution combine with his boat-angle to bring off the exercise successfully. The fine points of the maneuver will be honed later on when he plays in real rapids.

There are two kinds of Ferrying. The Backferry (or ferry glide) uses Back strokes to place and keep your boat in an advantageous position to sideslip as it points downstream roughly in the same direction as the current. The Upstream (or forward) Ferry uses Forward strokes to maintain a proper angle against the current and help propel your boat across the current.

When learning to Ferry, there are two basic principles to keep in mind: Always *angle your boat* slightly away from the direction of the current. And *always lean downstream,* regardless of the direction you're traveling: if you lean upstream the current will come down on your lowered gunwale and flip you over in an unplanned capsize. In addition, the downstream lean offers a larger surface area for the current to work on in helping you sideslip across the river.

By putting these principles together in a co-ordinated action you *and* the river join in a unique partnership to propel your kayak in the desired direction.

PINPOINTING DIRECTION

Up till now we've used clock numbers to designate the position of your paddle in relation to the bow of your kayak. Here, though, let's use the clock to show the direction your bow is pointing, and therefore your boat's angle in Ferrying.

Because there are no obstructions in the water we're practicing in, we will assume that the current flows straight down the river (rather than changing direction, as it does when rounding an obstacle in whitewater). Thus "downstream" and "current" will mean the same direction for simplicity's sake, and your bow will be at 12 o'clock as you go directly downstream with the current.

In the same way, when you point upstream straight into the current, your bow will stay at 12 o'clock.

BACKFERRY (FERRY GLIDE)

In a Backferry to the right while paddling downstream apply a couple of Back strokes on your left side to angle your boat toward 11 o'clock downcurrent. Then lean to the right (downstream) and apply a series of Back strokes on both sides of your boat to help maintain the correct angle as you sideslip across the current. You may have to paddle a bit harder on your right side in order to maintain correct boat-angle.

In a Backferry to the left, first angle your boat toward 1 o'clock downcurrent with a couple of firm Back strokes on the right side. Then lean to the left (downstream) and backpaddle briskly on both sides as you sideslip over to the left side of the river.

In an Upstream Ferry your boat must be headed roughly upstream, either because you are simply drifting downstream backward or you have just emerged from an eddy with your boat pointed upriver.

To ferry toward your right, first angle your bow toward 1 o'clock upcurrent, then lean to the right (downstream) and use several firm Forward strokes on both sides of your boat to maintain your correct angle to help propel your boat across the current. Again as in the Backferry, you may be required to paddle a bit harder on your right side in order to maintain correct boat angle.

In an Upstream Ferry to the left you simply angle your bow toward 11 o'clock upcurrent, lean downstream to your left, and use several Forward strokes to initiate and maintain your sideslip toward the other side of the river.

STABILIZING STROKES: THE PADDLE BRACES

Having learned the Half-roll via the Paddle-Brace Recovery and then the Eskimo Roll, you're well acquainted with the powerful leverage your paddle-blade can exert on the water. Now we're going to review the Brace on its own merits, and then see how it works forward, backward and to either side.

Braces are used not for propelling, but rather are to help you stabilize your boat and to make subtle directional changes. As your skill increases you'll rely more and more on your paddle-blade, extended way out from the boat, to give you more and more stability.

Forward Brace

In the Forward Brace on your way to the Roll you leaned to one side and slapped the face of the blade on the water near the bow. Then, as you began to tip over, you swung the blade out sideways and around from 1 o'clock to 3 o'clock. The leading edge of the blade is slightly raised at all times, preventing the blade from slicing downward through the water, thus losing its stabilizing "outrigger" effect.

In practicing the Forward Brace, keep leaning farther and farther each time until your head is immersed in the water and you can still recover.

Back Brace

The Back Brace stabilizes a kayak, and is also used quite naturally and without any formal training by neophytes who are simply

In the Back Brace—a stabilizing stroke—lean backward and slowly slide the rear blade in a short arc away from the boat on the surface of the water. (R.F.G.)

trying to steer their boats by holding their paddles on the water behind them.

The stroke consists of leaning backward and slowly pressing the rear blade—normally backside down—in a short arc on the surface of the water. By leaning to the right and sliding the blade from 5 o'clock to 3 o'clock, the Back Brace is completed on the right side. Sliding the left rear blade from about 7 o'clock to 9 o'clock on the left side will complete a Back Brace on that side.

The Back Brace changes to a Stern-rudder stroke if you change the paddle-angle from a flat to a vertical position in the water in order to help steer the boat.

The Brace and the Stern-rudder are highly useful strokes to have in your repertoire (particularly when coming in for a landing on shore), but they do slow your forward momentum. Therefore experienced paddlers soon wean themselves from the Stern-rudder and Back Brace, and use any number of Forward stroke combinations to make the kayak go in the desired direction without loss of speed.

The Side Brace

This stroke is used almost entirely as a means of stabilizing your boat rather than as a steering mechanism. If you feel unexpectedly unstable while moving forward, extend your right blade out on the water face down at 3 o'clock. Place the blade as far from the kayak as possible, with the leading edge slightly raised. Lean hard to your right with your left hand holding the rest of the paddle above your head. Surprisingly enough, you'll find that you're very stable in this position—just as much as when you are sitting quietly in a kayak in still water.

From the beginning of a Side Brace it is natural to move into a Draw by digging the blade into the water and pulling it in toward the boat. From a Side Brace you can also swing the blade forward in an arc toward the bow and then pull directly back, thus converting your Brace into a standard Forward stroke. You can also swing the blade back toward the rear of the kayak and transform your Side Brace into a Stern-rudder or Back stroke.

Slipping into a variety of strokes from the basic Side Brace can be an exhilarating complement to your kayaking style.

TWO GREAT TURNING STROKES

The proficient kayaker will often find good use for the spectacular Duffek stroke and the Cross-bow Draw. Both are turning maneuvers that utilize your forward momentum and your paddle as a pivot. And both are unusually effective in whitewater.

The Duffek

This great stroke revolutionized the sport of kayaking. It was developed by Milovan Duffek, a Czech kayaker who first demonstrated the move at the 1953 World Championships in Geneva. Ever since his innovation, kayakers have not had to rely on the boat itself for stability: the paddle becomes the primary means not only of support but also for *turning the kayak while in Brace position.*

What a nifty stroke it is—particularly in whitewater! But first learn the basic idea in flatwater; otherwise you'll spend a good share of the time upside down wondering what went wrong.

To simulate moving current in flatwater it is best to get going very fast—almost full speed in a forward direction. Then lean out as far as you can to the right. With the face of the blade at an angle of

A kayaker attempts a Duffek stroke to turn left into an eddy of quiet water behind a rock. The paddle acts as a pivot and spins the boat around. In this instance the bow has slipped too far past the rock, causing the paddler unnecessary effort to gain the eddy. (R.F.G.)

about 45 degrees to the forward direction of the boat, insert the blade at about 2 o'clock or approximately 3 feet away from the bow. Without stroking at all, hold your blade right there while your left hand is held high above your head. Presto!—the kayak will spin around to the right with the paddle acting as a pivot.

The exact blade-angle to use depends upon your speed, how far you lean, and how abruptly you wish to turn. The Duffek turn can often be finished with a firm but short Draw stroke to redress your balance.

If you wish to perform a Duffek turn to your left, simply hold your right hand high above your head and use your left hand to insert the left blade properly.

This is one of the most exciting moves in kayaking, but get the idea of it in flatwater, then try your luck in moving current, and then advance into eddies, etc. As an added bonus you'll be pleased that a Duffek properly done does not cut down your speed appreciatively.

In flatwater—on a lake or gentle river—you can come steaming up to a dock or other chosen point on the shore, pull a Duffek, and bring your kayak into a snappy landing right on the button. You'll have earned the right to hotdog it for the folks on shore.

Cross-bow Draw

If the Duffek pales with you, here's another move that is as stimulating as it is effective and abrupt.

While paddling forward hard, quickly swing the right blade over the bow and place it in on the *left* side in a Draw position about a foot away from the boat. This requires quite a bit of body twist at the waist. The blade enters the water almost in a vertical position—way forward at about 11 o'clock. Your left wrist will be slightly above your left ear, with your left elbow pointed comfortably out about 45 degrees. Your right elbow should be directly in front of you slightly below eye level.

Lean hard on the left, and pull the blade toward you; quickly the kayak will respond and snap around for you. The more you dare

A paddler uses a Cross-bow Draw to whip his boat around to the left. Note the excellent placement of the paddle. In this case, the kayaker is heading upstream; the current is moving from left to right. (L.C.C.)

to lean, the more effective the Cross-bow Draw stroke will be for you. Once the kayak has turned you can lift the paddle back across the forward deck and then smoothly execute a Forward stroke.

In order to do the Cross-bow Draw stroke to the right, simply extend your left blade over the deck to the right and go from there.

USING THE EXTENDED PADDLE

In automobiles we have a passing gear, which, when you press the accelerator to the floor, will give you an added surge of power; in a jet aircraft the afterburners are fired to boost the plane over the clouds or out of the enemy's reach. In kayaking we have the Extended Paddle technique, which, if used judiciously, can increase your quickness and maneuverability just when you need it the most. One of the most renowned practitioners of this art is former World Champion Jürgen Bremmer from the German Democratic Republic. Bremmer most often employs the extended blade in his Sweep strokes and Duffek turns.

Quite simply, the maneuver involves quickly sliding your hands along the paddle-shaft until one hand is at the throat of the paddle. The other hand remains halfway along the shaft, and the far end of the paddle will be the one in the water. This increases your leverage considerably. The net effect is to provide a temporary advantage of having a much longer paddle. Once the Sweep stroke or Duffek is completed, quickly slide the paddle back to its normal position in your hands.

One of the prettiest sights in kayaking is to watch a *Weltmeister* like Bremmer weave his way smoothly down through a slalom course subtly employing the extended paddle to increase his power and mastery over the rapids.

Other paddle and stroke techniques for other kinds of whitewater craft will be discussed by themselves before we cover whitewater technique.

5 *Technique for Other Craft*
[J . E .]

THE TECHNIQUES learned in a nimble little single-seater slalom kayak can also be applied to other closed-deck craft.

For whitewater racing the International Canoe Federation recognizes two other kinds of boats: the single-seater covered canoe (C–1), and the two-seater covered canoe (C–2).

But first let us consider the two-seater kayak (K–2), even though it is found more often on lakes and gentle streams than in rapids.

THE K–2

Years ago the K–2 was sometimes used for whitewater competition, but it has all but vanished now from the whitewater racing scene. There is probably not more than one K–2 for every 300 or so K–1's available in the United States, although it is popular in Europe as a Sunday-outing craft and in the British Isles. A highly specialized K–2, long and sleek and very tippy, is a legitimate flatwater racing class. In flatwater competition there is even a K–4—a magnificent boat to watch when all four paddlers are synchronizing their strokes.

For general recreational paddling purposes there are a couple of companies that manufacture the K–2 both in rigid fiberglass and also as a folding boat that can be dismantled in about 20 minutes and packed into two medium-large duffel bags for easy transport.

Applying Technique to the K–2

Whether the K–2 has one large cockpit accommodating two paddlers or separate cockpits fore and aft, and whether it is a collapsible folding-boat or made of fiberglass, the same paddling principles apply. Using the basic maneuvers we have learned, the bow and stern paddlers simply have to put these techniques together and synchronize their movements.

For the most part these K–2's are far more stable than the sassy little K–1's; designed for cruising, they therefore are not particularly fast or maneuverable boats. Because a K–2's main function is to go from here to there in a comfortable and pleasurable fashion—no quick turns in rough water, no standing on your ear to pivot around a rock—spray-skirts are not often used except while crossing windy lakes or in the ocean.

THE TRIM

Since two people paddle a K–2, it is important to consider the craft's trim. A stern-heavy boat wallows through the water and is sluggish to handle; a bow-heavy boat plows through the water and

Synchronizing their strokes, two kayakers paddle their wooden K–2 in the inland passage between Alaska and Seattle. These men are wearing spray-skirts, which are not always necessary in the stable K–2. (C.K.)

makes steering difficult. Therefore a K–2 when fully loaded should rest evenly on the water, neither bow- nor stern-heavy. If the heavier partner is in the bow, his seat should be moved back a little to compensate, just as one moves the heavier partner closer to the fulcrum of a seesaw to redress the balance. If the heavier partner happens to be the stern-man, then either the bow seat or the stern seat (possibly both) should be moved forward a bit. Only a couple of inches can make a big difference in the trim.

In a K–2 one person should be designated as "commander" before either paddler steps into the boat. It can be either the bow-man or the stern-man, but it usually turns out to be the more experienced boater of the two, or the owner of the boat. Customarily the bow-man steps in first while the stern-man holds the boat in position for him. Then, while the bow-man maintains the boat steady, the stern-man slips into the rear seat and announces that the K–2 is ready to get underway. In disembarking, the bow-man will step on shore first.

BOW AND STERN DUTIES

Most of the strokes that are used in the K–1 are also applicable to the K–2. Because the K–2 is a stable craft, it more commonly calls for the traditional forward, backward, and the simpler turning strokes, rather than relying so much on hanging (stabilizing) strokes.

As a general arrangement the paddling duties between the bow and stern divide themselves logically between forward power and steering, respectively. This does not mean, however, that the bow-man only provides power and the stern-man simply sits back and steers. It is logical for the bow-man to set and maintain the paddle-stroke rate since the stern-man can always see him, but he cannot always see the stern-man.

The stern-man, meanwhile, is the chief helmsman, and he will make frequent use of the Stern-rudder, the Draw, and the Sweep, always being careful to co-ordinate his strokes so he stays in rhythm with his partner in the bow. The stern paddler will provide his share of driving power with firm Forward strokes in rhythm with his partner.

A K–2 is rarely put into reverse, but when the need occurs both paddlers contribute toward backing up.

A good K–2 team must practice together conscientiously in order to combine their strokes for maximum effectiveness. For example, combining a bow Sweep on the right with a sharp Stern-rudder or stern Sweep on the left side will greatly aid spinning a K–2 toward the left.

Because K–2 paddlers often do not use spray-skirts, the Eskimo Roll is only rarely performed in a K–2. But if they do use spray-skirts, they follow K–1 procedures for Wet Exits or Rolls. Both paddlers should take care to synchronize the swing of their recovery Braces (and of course do them on the same side!).

THE C–1 IN WHITEWATER

This book does not deal with the activities of the open canoe in whitewater. Besides the K–1, the International Canoe Federation recognizes only closed-deck canoes for whitewater competition. Although the American Canoe Association sanctions open-canoe races, these are most often restricted to gentler whitewater of a nature more suitable for open boats, which are easily swamped in big rapids.

Comparisons with K–1

Because the canoeist's paddle is single-bladed, his maintainable stroke-rate is lower than that of the kayaker, who has two blades.

The canoe paddler kneels in his boat. By kneeling, he has a greater power center than the kayaker does: he can reach farther out into the water with his paddle for better control. Also, kneeling allows him more freedom to rotate his body than the seated paddler enjoys. Further, because the kneeling canoeist's head is about a foot higher than a kayaker's, he has the better forward visibility, which can be very important in fast-moving current.

HELPS FOR THE PADDLER

To keep his legs from becoming fatigued in kneeling, the paddler has a wooden crossbar (thwart) slung from just under each gunwale to rest his butt on.

So as not to allow his feet to slip around, a couple of wooden blocks are fastened to the floor of the canoe directly behind the thwart. These toebraces give the paddler something to push against and they act as chocks to keep his feet in place.

Even more important than the toebraces in keeping the paddler in efficient and comfortable position are the thighbraces, which prevent him from lurching forward. These thighbraces are usually straps whose lower ends are attached to the floor of the canoe on either side of the centerline and just in front of the thwart. Each upper end is attached to a gunwale to provide firm support for the inside of his thighs as he kneels.

WET EXIT AND ROLL IN A C-1

For a Wet Exit simply release the spray-skirt from around the coaming as you did in a K-1, and untuck your legs from the thigh-straps by lifting your feet up and away from the toebraces. As you drop clear of the boat remember to keep one hand on your boat and the other on your paddle.

The Eskimo Roll in a C-1 is very similar to the Broken Paddle Roll that we practiced in the K-1. Capsized (and kneeling), you reach for the surface with your paddle and make sure that the blade rests flat on the surface. In the Brace recovery, there is more emphasis on the bracing aspect and less emphasis on the sweep of the blade as it arcs along the water.

Don't forget the importance of hip-snap, and the fact that your head and shoulders should come up last.

CANOE STROKES

The Driving Strokes

The basic parts of the Forward stroke—dip, draw, recovery—in the canoe are similar to what we have already learned in the K-1.

The Forward stroke in a C–1 is similar to that stroke in a K–1: the dip (A), *the draw* (B), *and the recovery* (C). (R.F.G.)

In flatwater competition for C–1's the Forward stroke is of such overwhelming importance compared with other strokes that thousands of words have been written by experts dissecting all aspects of it. However, this book is focused on whitewater, so the fine points of an appropriate racing stroke for flatwater can be found elsewhere.

INDIAN STROKE

This stroke is a legacy from the Indians and was used to give them a silent approach to wild game or an enemy.

Instead of lifting your paddle out of the water at the end of a Forward stroke, you simply feather the blade so it will be parallel to the gunwale—its edge thus offering little resistance to the water—and draw the blade back through the water to the bow, where it is rotated back to its correct working position. You cannot get such a high stroke-rate this way as is possible in the conventional recovery of the blade through the air, but there is no sound of water dripping from the blade as it swings through the air, and no splash as it dips into the water to start the stroke. It is a silent, restful and smooth way to paddle.

BACK STROKE

For the simplest kind of Back stroke, place your blade behind you in the water and push it forward alongside your boat, using the back of the blade as the business side.

A second effective kind of Back stroke is the twist-pull-rotate-and-push combination that is spectacular to watch when done well. First, twist your body around so you are facing the rear of the boat. Insert the blade into the water with its face forward and pull it toward you alongside the boat. When it reaches your hip, rotate the paddle 180 degrees and in one smooth motion finish your Back stroke in the conventional way.

The Correcting Strokes

Since you stroke only on one side of the boat at a time, you must eventually compensate for the boat's natural desire to veer off-course away from the paddling side. Therefore there are two correcting strokes: the J stroke and the Pry. Both are almost unique to the canoe, thanks to the single-bladed paddle. Its short shaft and top hand-grip let the kneeling paddler really exert power where it is needed. The double-bladed kayak paddle is simply not as efficient in the J and Pry strokes, although some expert kayakers may use a modified form of the Pry.

THE J STROKE

The J stroke gets its name from the design the blade traces in the water as it completes a Forward stroke. On the left side of the boat it forms a conventional J, on the right side a J that has been flopped over.

If you look down on a canoe from above, the Forward stroke creates the upright part of the letter as the paddle moves alongside. Just prior to recovery, twist your blade a quarter-turn outward and push away as you remove the blade from the water. It is this outward curl of the J that brings the canoe back on course. When used best, it is a subtle motion, sometimes only for a couple of inches to keep the bow pointed straight ahead. It doesn't take much practice to determine how much of a curl you want on the J or to see that this stroke, used often, will prevent you from being forced to make big correcting strokes on the other side.

THE PRY

The Pry is a more vigorous version of the J stroke and can be thought of as tracing a smart right angle in the water.

At the end of the Forward stroke you give your blade a *brisk* quarter-turn outward (instead of a gentle outcurl); as you turn the shaft, press it hard against the gunwale—which acts as a fulcrum—and in one sharp motion use the blade to pry the boat sideways.

THE MINNESOTA SWITCH

Many North American paddlers use the Minnesota Switch to keep their boats on course, instead of repeated J and Pry strokes. In simplified terms it involves a series of strong, powerful Forward strokes on one side followed by an equal series of Forward strokes on the other side. This is accomplished by swapping your hand-grips as you switch the paddle in your hands from side to side.

On the whole, Europeans tend to scoff at the Switch, although

North American paddlers have had good luck with it. Maybe you have to be born to it. It gets its name because so many expert canoeists who have used it come from Minnesota.

THE C–2

The marvelously orchestrated teamwork of the whitewater C–2 is a joy to behold. Designed for rapids-running and whitewater racing, it has an entirely covered deck and is paddled by two people, one in the bow and one in the stern. Like the C–1, it has toe- and thigh-braces for the kneeling paddlers; its relatively flat, keel-less hull makes for quick turning.

Becoming a member of a C–2 team requires a very special kind of temperament. Like Siamese twins, you go where your partner goes whether you like it or not. The failure of one paddler's stroke in a C–2 can be critical, because the C–2 is a whitewater boat that requires split-second teamwork in order to meet the demands of the rapids.

One of the most exciting things to watch in all of sports is a well co-ordinated C–2 team weaving its way through a slalom course. Each man knows what his job is, and each man knows what his partner is doing. Every stroke and movement has been practiced and planned ahead of time. By combining their efforts—with a minimum of shouting and instructions—the canoe responds beautifully between them, spinning and pirouetting its way toward the finish line.

The International Canoe Federation recognizes the following personnel make-up for the canoe classes: C–1 means a single *man* in a canoe; C–2 means two *men* in the canoe; and C–2M means that the paddlers are one man and one woman.

With women playing an increasing role in all levels of sport these days, it was natural for them not to be limited solely to a K–1 or as the partner to a man in a C–2M class. In many of the races now held in the United States you can watch a woman paddling a C–1 or two women in a C–2. Although not recognized as official classes by the ICF there is nothing to prevent an innovative race organizer from offering a special C–1W or C–2W class.

A C–2 ferries across a stretch of whitewater. Precise teamwork between the two paddlers is the key. The C–2 is second only to the K–1 for speed in white-water. (R.F.G.)

C–2 Technique

You can think of a C–2 as a long, slender rectangle having four corners where the paddle can be applied basically to make the canoe respond to the will of its masters. At the bow there will be a right corner and a left corner as the bow-man kneels in position. Although the bow-man will choose whether he will paddle most of the time on the right or left side of the canoe, he must also have as part of his repertoire the spectacular Cross-bow Draw and similar movements that are performed on his off-side.

The stern provides two more corners. The stern-man normally will paddle opposite from the side the bow-man paddles on. Thus a symmetry of power and motion is provided, which helps to keep the boat going in a straight line. Occasionally the stern-man may also feel the need to switch over to his off-side in case extra power is needed there.

Bow and stern duties

The division of duties in a C–2 is not quite the same as for a K–2, where the stern-man was primarily the helmsman and the bow-man the power source. The stern-man is also concerned with using Draw, Sweep and Pry strokes whenever the need arises.

In the C–2 the bow-man has the responsibility for initiating turns. By using powerful Sweep and Draw strokes in which he can lean far out and away from the boat, he can help the stern-man materially with quick turns of direction. In addition, he will use a Pry effectively to push his boat sideways. Several quick Pry strokes have often made the difference between clear running down a rapids and being hung up on a rock. In whitewater slalom a quick, adroitly applied Pry has saved many a canoe from touching a pole.

No matter what strokes you use, the important thing is that as a C–2 team your strokes should be a continuous and integrated pattern, creating a steady power flow that seems to come from a single source. Thus two paddlers working as a team in a C–2 provide an efficient mechanism that makes the C–2 the fastest boat in whitewater next to the K–1.

THE SURFING KAYAK

Surfing with a board and riding similar waves in a kayak are two quite different sports. In a kayak you and your boat try to stick it out together when things don't go right. If the sea becomes unruly and tosses you about you always have a trump card up your sleeve: the Eskimo Roll. And since you are literally wearing your boat, it is possible for you to broadside a wave all the way in to a beach—as well as to ride the wave in backwards, and other tricks.

Best for surfing is the flat-bottomed kayak with seat well aft of center—a design now made commercially and sometimes called a Surfyak. However, any competent paddler can enjoy surfing in slalom or cruising kayaks, which have more rounded bottoms.

Technique

Place your kayak right at the water's edge pointing seaward. Simply shove your boat along by leaning forward and "poling" with your hands simultaneously on each side. Once waterborne, keep headed directly out to sea and paddle swiftly straight toward oncoming waves in deep water.

The foaming tip of a wave is its break-point, and it is this spot

A slalom kayak slides down the face of a wave. However, flat-bottomed surf kayaks made expressly for surfing are easiest to control as you ride in on a large wave. (OLD TOWN CANOE COMPANY)

that you will try to hit with your kayak. If you catch the wave at the right moment, you'll be on top of it, rushing toward the shore as white froth appears on either side of you. If you are ahead of the wave, simply paddle as hard as you can forward toward the beach, and the wave will catch up to you and give you a tremendous boost.

A curved-bottom kayak is likely to turn rather sharply to the right or left as you begin to ride in on a large wave. This turning is called *broaching*, and when it occurs, simply *lean hard into the wave* (seaward) and apply a high Paddle Brace back into the wave itself. Your kayak will slip along sideways in front of the wave, and you may get a ride all the way in to the beach.

When paddling toward shore on a large wave the bow of your kayak may drive under the surface toward the bottom. This is called *pearling*, and in deep water it can result in the boat falling forward end-over-end. When this happens you should lean forward, allow the boat to topple, wait a couple of seconds for the wave to break over you, and then right yourself with your reliable Eskimo Roll.

In shallow water, however, pearling can be dangerous, particularly if the bow digs into the sand. The kayaker should by all means lean forward to prevent back injury.

Safety

Kayak surfing is a relatively new sport and very little is known about handling a kayak in surf heavier than 8 feet. Leave big waves to the more experienced surfboarders. Be sure to check out the entire beach area well at low tide so you'll be familiar with any rocky ledges or underwater obstructions, and learn about the undertow. Make sure you'll avoid beds of seaweed: the plants can get tangled around your paddle.

The ocean will go relentlessly about its business if you get in difficulties, so *never surf alone*. Always go with a friend, even if it is simply someone standing by on shore. It is best, however, to avoid beaches where there are swimmers. They are not as agile in the water as a kayak and can very easily get in the way.

6 *Whitewater Technique*
[J . E .]

WATER on the move is nimble as well as subtle. It is apparently made up of an infinite series of layers that seem to slip over each other with very little friction. Running water is a truly dynamic medium, especially when temporarily obstructed by irregularities in the river-bed, by rocks in the way of its flow, or by unexpected twists and turns in the river.

A kayaker needs to know and become familiar with all the idiosyn-crasies of water on the move. Then will come the application of basic technique suited to each circumstance, and the exhilaration of whitewater paddling.

Reading the River

Water, in its headlong course toward the sea, carves for itself a highway that tries to take the path of least resistance across the surface of the land.

Basically there are three forces at work here: (1) gravity—which constantly lures water downward; (2) centrifugal force—which greatly affects a river as it swings around a bend and changes direc-tion; and (3) weight—because water while moving creates one of the strongest and most irresistible forces in all of nature.

If we could cut a riverbed crossways and examine the cut end

109

of either section, generally speaking we would notice the deepest portion of the river in the middle, with the water becoming more shallow as the sides of the riverbed slope up to meet the shore. Also, the fastest current can be found at the surface of the water in the middle part of the river. Toward the edges of the river, where the water becomes more shallow, there is greater friction for the volume of water, and the current slows down.

But there are notable exceptions to this simplified rule for current, and they are dictated by the terrain through and over which the river flows. The river paddler, however, heading smoothly down a slow-moving current, has little with which to concern himself. If he stays roughly in the middle of the river he'll get the benefit of the strongest current and deepest water the stream can offer.

Classification

Most traditional whitewater rivers are babbling and shallow bottom-scratchers much of the year. Such streams depend for whitewater on the spring run-off from melting snow. They rise and fall annually, earlier in the south and later in the north; the rivers that have substantial snow bases where they rise stay higher longer. Toward the end of the whitewater season a good rainfall will restore the water level of these rivers and temporarily prolong the season.

Whitewater rivers are classified in six general categories, with several factors determining classification: the complexity of the riverbed, the elevation drop per mile, the river's course, and the volume of water. The last factor—the volume of water—is the greatest variable and can alter a river's category dramatically.

Most beginning kayakers will be content with Class I and Class II water. Good whitewater touring is found in Class II and Class III. Rivers with stretches of rapids that fall into classes IV, V and VI—such as the great Western rivers—are for experts.

Class I.   Waves are little more than riffles. The current is slow to moderate. The course of the river is obvious. *Beginners' water.*

Class II.   Waves up to 1 foot high. Faster current. The course of the river is recognizable. *Requires basic whitewater skill.*

Class III.   Waves up to 3 feet. Fast current. The course of the river is passable but requires inspection because of boulders, holes and eddies. Class III is the limit for open boats. *Requires sound whitewater skills.*

Class IV.   Big, numerous waves. Very fast current. Careful inspection of the river's course is essential. *Requires advanced to expert level of skill.*

Class V.   Raging, roiling water with pounding waves. The violence of the rapids makes inspection mandatory. This water is almost beyond the realm of pleasure. *Requires absolute expertise.*

Class VI.   The extreme, so difficult that navigation is virtually impossible. *Even experts avoid this kind of water if possible.*

Heavy Water

Paddlers often use the expression "heavy water" or "big water" when describing a stretch of rapids that looks awesome. It would be misleading to define heavy water simply as anything over a certain number of cubic feet of water per second in a river, for there are at least three other variables to consider. The size of the riverbed, the degree of vertical drop, and the experience of the boater all must be taken into account.

In terms of the riverbed and water flow, it is reasonable to classify the Olympic slalom course at Augsburg as a heavy-water rapids, yet there is rarely more than 900 cubic feet per second pouring through its small, narrow bed. With a wider and bigger riverbed like that of the Housatonic in Connecticut, 900 cubic feet per second is barely enough to cover the rocks and float a boat.

For the novice, a Class III rapids may appear to be heavy water, whereas the expert might almost be bored by a "mere" Class III. As the rate of water-flow increases, however, more boaters will agree that it is, indeed, heavy water. Few would deny that the Mackenzie

CLASSIFICATION OF RIVERS

Classes I–V comprise the range of navigable water. Class VI rivers—worse than Class V, if you can believe it—are avoided even by super-kayakers. (W.R.)

CLASS I

CLASS II

CLASS III

CLASS IV

CLASS V

River in Canada or the Colorado River in the Grand Canyon is heavy water.

AROUND THE BEND

The simplest variation to deal with occurs when the river swings around a corner to head in a different direction. It is here that centrifugal force acts upon the water to create a lopsided river bottom, for here the deepest water will invariably be found near the *outside* edge of the river's bend. Novice river-runners will be tempted to "cut the corner" and thus save several yards, but the experienced paddler will swing wide, stay with the fastest water, and will beat the novice around the bend.

This is what whitewater kayaking is all about: high water on a fine spring day, and a kayaker heading toward the V *in a rapids.* (L.C.C.)

FASTER WATER AND ITS OBSTRUCTIONS

As a river quickens its pace, the fun begins. So watch sharply ahead and by observing carefully you will find that the water before you will form an inverted V in which the wide part is upstream and the pointed end, through which the current funnels, is downstream. Generally speaking, this inverted V in the water is a guide indicating where the main current is flowing, and where you want to go. A gentle yet perceptible descent can be felt at this point.

RIFFLES

When you pick up a little speed in the V as it narrows to its point, you'll notice ahead some small waves in the surface of the water. If the waves are not over a foot high they indicate a stretch of shallow water underneath. Such small waves are called *riffles*, and they are caused by an unevenness—submerged rocks, ledges, or sunken logs—in the riverbed below.

HAYSTACKS

Much larger standing waves—2 or more feet high—are often caused by huge submerged boulders, or they occur at the end of the chute of water from a V. These waves are called *haystacks*, and usually three or more come in succession. Haystacks in certain parts of the world on giant-sized rivers are so large that they appear to be hills of water in themselves.

ROCK GARDENS AND STAIRCASES

If the water level is low and the gradient fairly steep, the water will be churned up a bit and lots of little rocks will barely show their heads above the surface. Boaters will often call a section like this a *rock garden*. Navigation through a rock garden is tricky, and a paddler is lucky to get through one without at least once scratching the hull of his boat.

Another common river phenomenon is the *staircase*—a series of ledges or descending shelves over which the current spills. Again, the cautious paddler will search out the inverted V and follow, some-

A series of haystacks promises a challenging ride downstream (current flows away from viewer). Haystacks are often caused by huge submerged boulders. (L.C.C.)

times in a zigzag course, the flow of the greatest amount of current. Parts of the beautiful Shenandoah River in Virginia are famous for their staircase-like appearance.

EDDIES

Pockets of relatively still water can sometimes be found near either bank of the river or downstream of large exposed boulders or logs out in midstream. These pockets are called *eddies*, and they can be either benign or malicious.

The ones with relatively little current and which contain quiet water are great places to park and take a breather, and they are fine vantage points from which a camera buff can photograph oncoming paddlers as they plunge toward him down the rapids.

However, not all eddies can be considered friendly or as places to

The current (flowing from left to right) creates a giant eddy (dark water) where it flows around a rock outcrop. Strong, frothing jets pour past on either side, but the kayaker can sit quietly in the protected eddy. (L.C.C.)

linger for long. Owing to complex hydraulic phenomena working on the irregularities of a riverbed, an eddy can provide some nasty water for the unsuspecting kayaker. Often water will boil up, swirl and twist about—even forming whirlpools—making such an eddy unpredictable as well as unpleasant as a rest stop. You feel as if some underwater monster had reached up and grabbed the hull of your boat, taking fiendish delight in yanking you from one side to another. This type of eddy is no place to relax or loiter, but well-executed Braces will stabilize your boat, and several strong Forward strokes will take you out into the mainstream again.

One of the most famous of malicious eddies is the one just below the formidable Avery Brundage Rock on the upper part of the 1972 Olympic whitewater slalom course in Augsburg, West Germany. Another eddy well known to paddlers lies just below the Dumplings on the West River in Vermont. At both places the unstable water has lured photographers, because it is here that the unsuspecting boater will provide the camera with some potentially spectacular coverage.

THE ANATOMY OF AN EDDY

In general, as the current diverges around an obstacle, it forms a very fast and powerful chute, or jet, that skirts past the head of the eddy, which lies immediately below the obstruction. The characteristic circular motion of the eddy is created in part by the passage of the jet: this milder countercurrent in the surface water of the eddy curves inward and upstream; then, when it meets the obstacle at the eddy's head, it peels off and heads downstream.

A sharp delineation can be seen between the chute roaring downstream and the more placid eddy water. This is called the *eddy-line.*

A short eddy-wall is sometimes formed at the top of an eddy right on the eddy-line if the chute (jet) of downstream water is of unusually heavy volume and force. There can be a difference of a foot or more in this wall between the eddy water and the chute next to it.

A couple of boat lengths downstream is an area often called the eddy-tail. Here the chute fans out and loses some of its force, which causes the eddy water itself to lose its upstream momentum; and the river water merges again.

EDDIES AT THE SIDE OR MIDSTREAM

All kinds of interesting things are happening near the riverbank as a river picks up speed and descends more sharply. Quite common is the *side-eddy,* caused by the jut of a large boulder or point of land

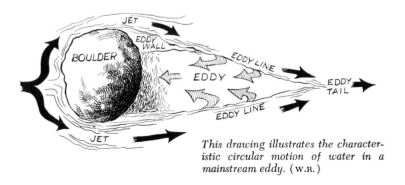

This drawing illustrates the characteristic circular motion of water in a mainstream eddy. (W.R.)

into the main stream, leaving a space downstream of it where water can swirl back and return in an upstream circular motion.

A side-eddy can be a welcome haven. It is an automatic "parking place" while you plan your next move downstream; it can provide ready access to shore and a chance to get out to stretch; and it's a very good place for putting-in at the start of a river journey.

A side-eddy offers many opportunities to practice precision boating or just a chance to play around. And it is also a likely place to find lost paddles or other debris. The most feasible way to search for lost gear is to scout out each side-eddy carefully as you proceed downriver.

Below—downstream of—a big exposed boulder will lie a midstream eddy. Such an eddy will often have not only a jet or chute roaring past on *either* side of the boulder, but will also have an eddy-wall and an eddy-line on either side of the eddy. Between these lines and directly below the boulder you'll find relatively stable, quiet water moving upstream back toward the rock.

A midstream eddy offers you a choice of moving out either from the right or the left as you proceed down the rapids, and a careful examination of the next 100 yards or so below the eddy from a position of safety in the eddy itself will give you a clue as to which side you may wish to leave the eddy from.

ROLLERS/STOPPERS AND SOUSEHOLES

Among the other demanding obstructions to watch for in rapids are rollers (also called stoppers), souseholes (suckholes), reversals, or just plain "holes."

Regardless of what you call them, however, they all share one basic characteristic: water at the base of the obstruction is being tossed about in a backlash, thrashing opposite to the natural downstream flow of the current.

Although there may be some technical differences in these terms, they are used somewhat interchangeably according to the section of North America you happen to be paddling in. No really precise definitions are necessary because Nature can, in her own way, provide an almost infinite variety of challenges in a stretch of rapids.

An obstruction in the river (current flows from left to right) creates a souse-hole. The water hits the hole and curls back on itself, creating a trough that can stop the downstream motion of a kayak. (L.C.C.)

It is enough to be able to recognize that these things do exist in turbulent waters and, after recognizing them for what they are, to know what to do about them.

ROLLERS/STOPPERS

Turbulence that is called a roller or stopper is a tricky wave that remains in the same place athwart the river, and is formed by water plowing over a large obstruction and plunging down into a trough. The term "stopper" has been applied to rollers because that is exactly what the roller is likely to do to your boat if you linger too long in its vicinity. If you get in the trough, the roller can actually *stop* your forward motion downstream and keep you penned up for a while.

A roller is studied much more easily if you look upstream at it from the safety of the riverbank rather than from the cockpit of a kayak heading downstream. It can be fairly small and localized or it can extend most of the way across the river.

At the Quarter Mile Rapids on the White River in Vermont during unusually high water, a truly delightful roller extends diagonally all the way across the river. Another famous and challenging roller is located on the River aux Sables in the northern part of Quebec in Canada, about halfway down the slalom practice area near Jonquière.

THOSE HOLES

Souseholes, suckholes or reversals are formed in nearly the same way as a roller or stopper, except that they are often concentrated in one central spot in the river rather than extending across the stream. They too are formed by a huge boulder or ledge, but can also be formed by a weir or dam.

The water, as it plunges over the obstacle, divides itself into two main components: (1) the water that goes deep and continues on downstream, and (2) the part that is deflected back upstream toward the obstacle, creating a foaming, boiling backlash. To the unwary it looks like the jaws of a water monster—and a sousehole deserves respect from every paddler.

A sousehole may contain a roller as part of its composition, depending upon the river's configuration at the moment, and a roller can have as part of its repertoire the makings of a sousehole.

WEIRS AND DAMS

There are very few rivers within easy reach of civilization that are not obstructed by at least one dam or weir, and this is one of the reasons why every competent paddler scouts an unfamiliar stream before undertaking to travel it.

A weir is a small dam up to about 5 feet in height, and sometimes it has a sluiceway at one side to conduct the water to a mill or pond. In both dams and weirs, the water spills over almost vertically and usually creates immediately downstream a roller or sousehole, which in turn tends to toss back toward the barrier any debris that has floated over it.

When you look downstream at a dam or weir you see a "horizon line" ahead on the surface of the water. This occurs because the water usually is backed up against the barrier and the water is likely to be calm there without much current. Then, as the water goes over the dam, it creates a straight horizontal line across the river—as if

The arrows indicate a "horizon line"—an immediate signal to pull to shore and inspect the hidden dam or weir that undoubtedly lies just below the line. (L.C.C.)

the river simply stops and drops off the earth. Larger dams, of course, have superstructures on either side of the river—and sometimes all the way over the river—making identification easier.

Every boater should always be on the lookout for these horizon lines across the river ahead, and should pull over to shore immediately to scout out the dam *before* running it. And then, run it only with the greatest of caution, and preferably with a rescue party to assist you from shore.

Running Rapids

Some sports are designed mainly for one purpose: competition. Kayaking, however, is a versatile pastime, offering plenty of chances for self-expression. Compete if you wish. Or just go out with a few friends and run the rapids on a beautiful day. What's even better is to combine these activities. It is a common sight to see a group of slalomists practice hard on a certain stretch of the rapids for an hour or so, then suddenly peel off down the rapids in wild abandon, shouting to each other as they automatically size up what is approaching and then making the appropriate moves for the occasion.

Up till now your technique has been polished in flatwater, and you have learned what a nimble little craft you have under you. Now with the Eskimo Roll and basic strokes mastered, you are ready to enter the exciting world of whitewater.

But kayaking through the rapids should be much more than a simple, bouncy ride interspersed with a few unexpected thrills. A Sunday afternoon thrill-seeker who is ill equipped and ill prepared can often be a menace to the sport as well as to himself. Such an adventurer's inability to read the river is mirrored in his perplexed expression as his face emerges spouting water after his craft has capsized.

On the other hand, instead of "shooting" the rapids mindlessly just for an instant's worth of thrill, the true paddler will study the rapids carefully and then weave his way down, following a plan more well-thought-out than merely hoping to stay upright and dry.

Working over a stretch of whitewater with a sporty little kayak can be a very fulfilling experience. It's a real thrill to *know* a river well enough to use its currents, eddies, and waves to choreograph your pivots, spins and glides as your boat dances through the water.

SAFETY MEASURES

To save yourself embarrassment and possible loss of your boat or paddle, or even your life, adhere to the following without fail:

1. You must be a strong, competent swimmer; and you should never go river-running with anyone who isn't a good swimmer too.

2. If you value your life as well as your boat, you'll never kayak alone in rapids. Two boats are a minimum for safety; three are better.

3. No unknown rapids should ever be run without being scouted beforehand, and maps should be studied with care. Know what you are getting into: there are bound to be stretches where it's mighty difficult, even for experts, to reach the haven of an emergency take-out spot on the riverbank.

4. In addition to the lifejacket and helmet that you always wear, in cold weather it is smart to wear at least part of a wet-suit too, lest you find yourself helpless in the grip of cold water. Water below

50 degrees Fahrenheit will soon sap the energy of the strongest man.

5. Have adequate flotation in both bow and stern so your boat will ride high in the water in case of a capsize. This mean flotation bags: half-inflated beach balls, casually stuffed inside your boat, are not enough.

6. Grabloops at each end of the boat are also essential. With them your boat can be quickly controlled and pulled to shore in case of a capsize.

RULES-OF-THUMB

Intelligent rapids-running involves a continuous mental exercise to interpret the demands of the water as the river unfolds in front of you.

Actually "playing the river" involves two distinct things: (1) recognizing what it is you are approaching in the rapids, and (2) anticipating the appropriate move for the occasion.

DEEP WATER

Generally speaking, the deepest water will lie in the middle of the now familiar inverted V of glassy water where the main current is flowing.

When the river is going around a bend, however, the water will be deepest on the *outside* of the turn.

KEEP GOING

When in doubt or startled it is best to paddle hard *forward* rather than to try to back off with backward strokes. Never hoist your paddle above your head in despair: an "air brace" provides no stability.

LEAN DOWNSTREAM

When playing in the rapids always remember to *lean downstream*. This is probably the single most important rule in all of rapids-running.

It is highly unlikely that you will ever capsize if you remember always to lean downstream while maneuvering in rapids. However, the moment you get careless and allow your upstream gunwale to dip, the force of the water will grab your gunwale—and over you'll go.

Experienced boaters often refer to this phenomenon in terms of mythology. Old river-runners will tell you about an underwater creature called The Muncher that lurks in the rapids and likes to punish boaters who disobey the basic fundamentals of river-reading. The Muncher will spin your boat around if you don't pay strict attention to the currents and, if The Muncher is unusually hungry, he might even tip your boat over in the rapids. But you can always foil the critter by careful water-reading, by leaning downstream, and by having a reliable Eskimo Roll.

DEALING WITH HAYSTACKS

Soon after entering a rapid you are likely to encounter a series of those large standing waves called Haystacks. If they are not too large for your taste you may wish to smash straight through them for a real roller-coaster ride downriver.

If they appear more ominous than hospitable, steer slightly to one side using a Draw or Sweep stroke or even a Stern-rudder, and skirt the heavier haystacks lurking in the middle.

Haystacks don't have to be confronted from a straight forward position either. It is perfectly acceptable to approach them broadside—just so long as you always remember to lean and brace downstream.

Riding haystacks backwards can also provide a thrill, but you'd better know what lies downstream of them, or you'll be in for a surprise.

USING EDDIES

Your greatest ally in the rapids is an upcoming eddy.

Let's say that you have spotted a side-eddy to your right a hundred yards ahead downstream, because—from the configuration of the land or a boulder—you can anticipate the location of an eddy before it is clearly visible from your boat. Head toward it, driving hard with firm Forward strokes, always bearing in mind that the jet (chute) just alongside the eddy will tend to carry you downstream farther than you expect. Therefore aim for a point higher upstream in the eddy than you really plan to go.

Keeping paddling hard forward toward the eddy-line and into the eddy-water itself. As the eddy-line extends under your boat about halfway to your cockpit, you'll begin to feel the upstream eddy-water begin to grab your bow and force your boat around so that it is pointing upstream in the eddy.

Strokes for Entering an Eddy

A combination of strong Forward strokes, coupled at the last minute with a strong Sweep, will propel your boat into an eddy.

Or a favorite stroke to use here is the Duffek. The most common error, though, it to begin the Duffek stroke too soon. If you perform the Duffek too far away from the eddy proper, or in the jet itself, your boat will simply wash downstream and miss the eddy entirely. Resist beginning the Duffek until you can practically lean over and place your paddle-blade in the calmer water, *beyond* the eddy-line. This takes skill and good timing.

At the precise moment your boat leaves the downstream jet and actually enters the eddy you should shift your weight so as to lean *away* from the eddy. Centrifugal force plus the upstream current in the eddy will tend to pull you over, so counteract this by leaning back toward the main current of the river. A little practice will give you the feel for what to do. Don't get discouraged if you tip over several times while entering an eddy, because proper anticipation and timing take a lot of experience. But once learned, this maneuver is a pleasurable one.

Leaving the Eddy

Once in the eddy you'll have time to gather your wits and decide how to proceed out of the eddy and get on your way down the rapids.

First, look downstream and decide where you want to go, then

A

B

C

This unique series of action photographs shows a kayaker entering a mainstream eddy and then maneuvering into a side-eddy. He heads straight down
through the jet (A), then begins his turn to reach the quiet eddy behind the
big rock (B), using Forward strokes and the force of the jet to finish the eddy

turn (C). *In the eddy, he turns the kayak and prepares to ferry across the river* (D). *An Upstream Ferry* (*with the kayak at the proper angle*) *carries him across the current* (E), *and he slides neatly into a side-eddy* (F). (R.F.G)

choose which of three possible exits from the eddy is best for you. One way is simply to drift below the eddy-tail as you slowly turn to head downstream; if there are no obstructions directly downstream of the eddy-tail, this is probably the easiest way to leave an eddy. Or you can choose to peel off from about halfway up the eddy; or you can continue up the eddy and peel off dramatically just inches below the rock at the head of the eddy.

THE PEEL-OFF

The peel-off is a spectacular maneuver that can be done forward or backward.

To get ready to peel off to the right, you consider directly upstream as 12 o'clock. Back down the eddy as far as you can, to get a running start; then charge full steam ahead up the eddy with your *bow pointing between 1 and 2 o'clock*. The moment your bow crosses the eddy-line into the jet of fast-moving current you should continue to paddle hard and at the same time *lean hard downstream*. (It is at this point that one of the cardinal rules of whitewater kayaking will be driven home to you: lean downstream. Otherwise, the moment your bow hits that fast water you'll be upside down as quick as a wink.) The closer your bow points toward 2 o'clock the greater the chances that you'll spin quickly out of the current in an exhilarating manner and head down the river again.

For a left-side peel-off, back down for a running start, then plow forward fast with your bow somewhere *between 10 and 11 o'clock*. Lean downstream as you hit the jet, and let the current complete your turn to the left.

Peel-offs can be done backward as well as forward. Simply turn your boat around and, by using several firm Back strokes, move out of the eddy with your stern pointing between 1 and 2 o'clock if you're intending to peel off to the right (or pointing between 10 and 11 o'clock if you're peeling off to the left). Either way, you'll spin around and find yourself out in the current facing upstream. And in certain situations it could be more desirable to be facing upstream.

THE CARTWHEEL

It is fun as well as good practice to leave and then re-enter the same eddy at almost the same spot. This is called *cartwheeling*. For

The peel-off makes a spectacular exit from an eddy. The kayaker first backs his boat toward the tail of the eddy, then paddles ahead full speed at a slight angle toward the jet (A). As his boat enters the jet of fast water he keeps paddling and leans hard downstream (B). The current catches the kayak and completes the turn (C). (R.F.G.)

a cartwheel to the right, take off from the top of an eddy forward at about 2 o'clock (considering 12 o'clock as directly upstream), lean hard downstream and then, with a couple of Sweep strokes on the left side, guide the bow of your kayak back across the eddy-line into the eddy again. The main force of the current in the jet will then catch your stern and swing it around until you find yourself safely parked in the same eddy again facing upstream.

For a cartwheel to the left, point your bow at 10 o'clock; continue as above. Cartwheels can very quickly become a game between two kayaks to see which can make the tightest turn and lose the least amount of downstream position. It is also fun to try to see who can do a cartwheel with the least number of Sweep strokes.

Trying cartwheels both forward and backward out of eddies from both right and left can work wonders in improving your skill in boating. What's more, it will give you a real feel for the eddy-line, the power of the jet, and for the eddy itself. Good cartwheelers can spin out of an eddy, sweep quickly around and cut back into the eddy at almost the same place, all with very little loss of position.

FERRYING

Ferrying is basic to safe navigation in whitewater, and the trick is to get the massive forces of nature to do the work for you. I once saw former World Champion Jürgen Bremmer peel off out of a side-eddy on the Passer River in Italy and ferry across the entire river using only one stroke. A clever ferry-man can actually work his way upstream in the rapids by judicious use of ferry techniques and eddy-hopping (which we'll try in a minute).

Backferry (Ferry Glide)

If you want to move laterally across at least part of the river while moving downstream in strong current you can use the Backferry (sometimes also called the Ferry Glide).

Suppose you are heading down through rapids and see an obstruction ahead that you'd like to avoid—for example, a rock dead ahead with a clear passage to the right at 1 o'clock.

Your first and natural inclination is to point your bow to the right at 1 o'clock and paddle hard toward the clear passage.

However, the current may be stronger than you think, and your defensive efforts are coming too late. So stop paddling forward, point your bow to 11 o'clock diagonally away from the direction you want to go, and then employ several strong Back strokes while leaning downstream. The angle you have created with the boat and the water, plus the force of the current against the slowed boat, will work wonders for you.

After you have side-slipped over as far as you want, you can straighten your boat out with a forward Sweep stroke so you are pointing straight downstream again. Ferry Glides both to the right and to the left are standard moves any good kayaker uses in picking his way down a rapid.

The Upstream Ferry

Equally challenging is the Upstream Ferry. This is usually begun by driving hard out of an eddy upstream at an angle of not more than 1 o'clock or 11 o'clock—depending on which direction you want —while maintaining firm Forward strokes and a distinct downstream lean.

Getting the right angle and thrust so you'll slip across the river will take a bit of patience and practice. Here are two likely mistakes and how to avoid them.

First, if your boat keeps turning downstream like an unmanageable horse, this means that your angle of exit from the eddy is too close to 3 o'clock if you are moving out to the right, or too close to 9 o'clock if you are moving out to the left. Make sure your bow is pointed *not more* than 1 o'clock for a Ferry to the right, or 11 o'clock for a Ferry to the left.

Second, if your boat ferries out nicely about halfway and then stops moving laterally across the river, the chances are your bow has crept back toward 12 o'clock. Allow it to fall off *slightly* toward 11 or 1 o'clock while paddling forward, and your Ferry will begin again.

Eddy-hopping Upstream

Most people think of rapids as something for a boat to go *down* through. Yet salmon go up very swift streams in search of spawning grounds, and by borrowing a few ideas from these denizens of the river we too can work our way upstream. If the rapids are not too severe and a variety of eddies abound, it is great fun to test your skill in eddy-hopping *up* the river.

Start from one eddy and move up to its head, then charge hard out of it and ferry, maintaining strong Forward strokes, over to the tail of an eddy on the other side of the river. Work your way up from the tail of this eddy to its top—where you look for the next eddy upstream.

In a way, eddy-hopping can be compared to crossing from the head of one ski lift to the bottom of another farther up the mountain as you hitch to the topmost run of an alpine ski area. In this case the eddy acts as your ski lift—with the added bonus of having no lift lines or tickets.

PLAYING IN ROLLERS

A roller can flip you over quickly if you're unprepared—as explained earlier—but a roller can also provide some wonderful opportunities for exciting whitewater boating. An entire afternoon can be spent at one single place in whitewater that has a good roller with accessible eddies on either side.

If you turn around and back slowly down into a roller you'll soon feel the exciting sensation of having your stern rise high behind you as your bow disappears underwater at the bottom of the trough below the roller. At this moment you may start to swerve right or left, but with a good Paddle Brace you can correct your position nicely to avoid getting broadside. However, if you *do* become broadside in a roller, follow your natural tendency to do a high Paddle Brace—that is, bracing with an extended blade—on the downstream side, and you'll be perfectly O.K.

Sometimes the roller will shoot you straight back into the air.

In other cases you will do a modest loop-the-loop or "ender," winding up upside down. In any event simply be patient when you find yourself capsized, and Eskimo Roll back up.

A roller enjoys keeping kayaks broadside to the current so they can be bounced around a bit. If it is a worthy roller it will challenge your ability to get out of its clutches. In small rollers the high downstream side Paddle Brace is enough to pull you out. If not, then you should combine the side Paddle Brace with a couple of strong Forward or Back strokes: these will force you to the side of the roller. At this point, as if in disgust, the roller quite likely will spit you out into an eddy or into the main portion of the river.

More daring is coasting forward downstream into a roller—but meanwhile back-paddling strongly, so your boat slowly sinks into the roller itself. Then lean back until you feel your stern go deep into the trough and finally get caught by the strongest downstream current, which moves you straight downstream standing on your tail.

Modest end-over-ends can be done this way as your stern literally goes under while your bow sticks high into the air. Again, when this happens, simply wait a moment or two underwater, then complete your Eskimo Roll to right yourself again.

With a handy eddy on either side of a roller it is fun to head upstream from one eddy toward another by skimming across the top of the roller with your bow just missing the trough. Usually this creates one of the fastest Upstream Ferries imaginable.

Rollers with no dangerous rocks underneath can be places to strut your stuff with an Eskimo Roll. Better yet, I've seen some experts on the Farmington River at Tariffville Gorge in Connecticut do numerous Eskimo Rolls while broadside in that roller—hands-only Rolls at that, because they have thrown away their paddles!

On many of the really big rivers large rolling waves will be seen. Try an Upstream Ferry out to the top of such a wave, then keep your bow pointed toward 1 or 11 o'clock while facing upstream. Lean slightly downstream and the big current forcing up against your hull will slide your kayak neatly across the surface of the wave. By shifting his weight and controlling his boat, a good paddler can glide back and forth several times on the same wave.

PLAYING IN SOUSEHOLES

Souseholes (suckholes or reversals)—even though they may be part of the roller complex in a stretch of rapids—should always be approached with great caution. The smaller, safe ones are fun to play in, but large souseholes should be avoided by everyone except the most expert boaters. When considering souseholes as are found on the Colorado River in the Grand Canyon or the Bull Sluice on the Chattooga River, even top-notch paddlers wear—just in case—the big 33-pound buoyancy lifejacket rather than the lighter racing vest, which does not provide nearly as much flotation.

Of course every competent boater wears a helmet in rapids, and the importance of this protective headgear is demonstrated in souseholes. The "jaws" of a sousehole can catch you quickly, making for a very speedy capsize in all that frothy foam, which can conceal a variety of lurking obstructions.

Good boating sense dictates that you stay away from big souseholes in general, and start with the smallest ones before working your way up to larger holes as you gain knowledge of the powerful hydraulics involved.

Entering a hole

If you wish to play in the smaller souseholes, try nosing down into the hole in a forward position, meanwhile making Back strokes in order to travel slower than the rate of the current.

Another approach is to sneak from an eddy on either side into a sousehole. Move diagonally upstream out of the eddy with strong Forward strokes, and dive into the sousehole. More daring boaters may wish to drop down into a sousehole backward or sideways.

Once into the hole your boat will be buffeted and bounced around a bit and will very likely turn diagonally one way or another: *At this point always remember to lean and brace downstream.*

Small or reasonably-sized souseholes offer splendid opportunities to learn boat control. A truly expert boater can stick his bow or stern directly into the center of a sousehole and force the onrushing water to spit his boat straight back—sometimes even into the air. Or, if driven in deep enough, the bow or stern will be caught by the powerful water beneath the surface and the kayak will be forced to go end over end, which can be one of the greatest thrills in kayaking.

A more constructive procedure is to use several firm Forward strokes to augment a downstream Brace when you are ready to exit from a sousehole. Or, sometimes it is more convenient to blend that downstream Brace with several firm Back strokes to back your boat out of the hole.

DEALING WITH LARGER HOLES

In really heavy water (anything over 2,000 cubic feet per second) that offers the likelihood of powerful souseholes, there are basically two schools of thought concerning procedure. The first emphasizes that a boater should—contrary to his natural instincts—paddle *hard* right through the hole itself. Here you'll have to make yourself keep paddling, but the force of your momentum augmented by the power of your strokes will see you through.

A second school of thought believes that you should relax and take it easy. Allow your boat to float along the downstream current and do not take any aggressive action at all *until* you are in the very heart of the sousehole: at that point lean and Brace on your downstream side. Practitioners of this art love to drop into souseholes or ride giant haystacks in a sideways or even backward position. It really doesn't make much difference in what direction the boat is heading as it drops into the hole, because you then can play or exit, as you wish.

ABOUT RUNNING WEIRS AND DAMS

It is a common thing these days to see photographs of kayaks actually airborne as they sail over weirs and dams.

To the unwary thrill-seeker this may look like the ultimate in boating. It is more likely to be an invitation to trouble.

Running a weir or a dam will inevitably cause undue stress to your boat—one that it was never designed to take. In addition, the impact of hitting the water below the dam at an awkward angle can create a physical shock to the person in the boat, possibly injuring his spine or neck. And, finally, the backwash of water just down-stream can pin the paddler and his boat in its grip. He then must be rescued from shore with his boat perhaps abandoned and battered to pieces against the foot of the barrier.

In general, therefore, do not run dams and weirs unless there is a sluiceway provided. Portage instead. The momentary thrill of going over the steep pitch of water is negated by the variety of dangers involved.

7 *Cruising*
[R . R . A .]

WE PUT our kayaks in the river on a Sunday morning late in May before anyone was stirring. The dun-colored early morning rain clouds were blowing away as the two of us paddled from shore toward the mile of flatwater we would warm up on before the river really began to run.

The chill off the river began to disappear as the cloud cover slid by the sun. A strident blue sky was to bless the rest of the day. The friendly, familiar West River of Vermont that carried us now behind a white clapboard village was near the end of its spring run-off, so this might be the next-to-last run we would make this year. When we stopped paddling and dipped our fingers in the river, the bone-chill of real whitewater was gone. Already the banks showed signs of drying out now that the water level had dropped. Matted grass at the river's edge was turning green and the muddy bushes were tangled with the debris of broken branches floated down by the high water of mid April. Ahead, around the bend, the usual pounding roar of the first stretch of fast water had definitely diminished since the last run two weeks before. Now the river looked more rock-strewn as the dry tops of boulders poked through the current.

It was a fine, relaxed five-mile run. We could afford to be casual. The river's temperature had moderated and on a sunny day, turning hot as this one would, a dunking would be pleasant enough. Just bathing suits today, no clammy wet-suit anymore. We took the kayaks out once to sit in the warming sun and watch the river spill

A covey of kayaks cruises down Vermont's West River near Jamaica during a water release by a dam upstream. (R.F.G.)

over and around the midstream boulders. In the stretches of flat-water between the rapids we unfastened our helmets and leaned back, letting the kayaks turn lazily broadside. Above us on the hillside were farms with red barns and apple trees beginning to show some blossoms.

Three miles downstream an island squeezed the river, sending waves cascading off the rock wall on the bankside and tumbling back down upon the churning main current. We ran this hollering, then spun out of the current at the end of the island. We beached, and portaged the kayaks on our shoulders along the stone shore of the island to make that irresistible run once more.

We took the kayaks out a mile farther down, just below the covered bridge where the river makes a final roller-coaster drop. We scrambled the boats up a steep bank to the road 50 feet above the river, and hung out a thumb. . . .

For most people this sort of day trip is what whitewater kayaking is all about. But when time permits, the one-day paddle can expand to a weekend or week-long camping trip. Beyond that lies the realm of wilderness whitewater rivers—particularly the great ones of the West.

This chapter deals first with getting the beginner into a club, for here lies the fastest, easiest, and safest route to whitewater pleasure. Then it deals with finding whitewater rivers suitable for your level of ability, whatever it may be. Finally, there are suggestions for the basics of day trips, camping trips, and wilderness river trips.

HOW TO GET STARTED

Many major cities have well-established kayak clubs, although if the club is an older one it may be called a canoe club. Clubs increas-

Whitewater clubs embrace many sizes and styles of river craft. Here, members of a New England club set off in kayaks, closed-deck canoes, and open canoes for a day trip. (R.F.G.)

ingly are providing facilities for building boats, and many offer indoor-pool sessions during the winter months. A club can steer you to the right river for your degree of ability and provide the companions who are vital to safe kayaking. To find a club ask at a local wilderness outfitting store. They usually know. Or you can write to the two national organizations: The American Canoe Association and the American Whitewater Affiliation, whose addresses are in the list of whitewater clubs in the Appendix.

If there is no kayak club near by, talk with people in an outing group or conservation society. Many—such as the Appalachian Mountain Club in the Northeast and the Sierra Club in the West—have active whitewater programs in their spring agenda.

Or if you know a kayaker in your area you may be able to persuade him or her to give you some instruction. If all this fails and you're stuck, you'll just have to learn from this book.

WHERE'S THE WATER?

Virtually every navigable river in the United States has had someone run its length and write the story of the adventure. Some accounts are pure harumscarum, written by bananas who should have stayed on the riverbank. But real whitewater people have built up a valuable body of river literature that makes recreational whitewater touring a much safer and more pleasurable sport.

GUIDEBOOKS

There have always been a few reliable regional guidebooks and maps to the whitewater rivers. In the last few years, in response to the public's growing interest in conservation and in river touring, a number of books and guides have been published and more are being written. A *good* book will include put-in and take-out points, significant mileages, water difficulty, notable landmarks, and the best times of year for touring. There are a few inadequate river guides, though, so if a book doesn't have at least this basic information, don't rely on it (who knows?—the author may have overlooked a waterfall or two).

MAPS

The United States Geological Survey maps are primarily useful in locating access and egress points, noting elevation changes, and showing dams en route. You cannot rely solely on these maps, however, or on any single map except the one for your particular river.

As a matter of course you should scout *any* river thoroughly before trying it for the first time. Fortunately, road-builders prefer river valleys, and often much of a river can be seen from a car. But get out on foot to inspect anything unusual.

WATER RELEASE

Some dams periodically release water to meet the needs of industries downstream. Others release water in the autumn to provide storage room for the following spring's run-off. Many whitewater races are held on rivers that are dam-controlled because, the authorities willing, a dependable amount of water can be counted on for race day. If the river you pick is dam-controlled, it's a good idea to ask the owner of the dam for the release schedule and the quantity of water (measured in cubic feet per second) that will be let out.

RIVER CLASSIFICATION

A description of the standard classification—ranging from I to VI according to degree of difficulty for the boater—is presented early in the preceding chapter on whitewater technique.

Further, any reliable whitewater guide applies these classifications to rivers most likely to be paddled.

And, for less-known and out-of-the-way streams, clubs or individual kayakers in the area can tell you what class of water you're likely to encounter, and where variations occur along the stretch you plan to cruise.

Being realistic about your own whitewater expertise—as well as the ability of others in your party—is of course the first consideration in planning a trip of any length. Then use classifications to help you select the river for your outing.

Kayaking is so darn much fun that it's a shame to save the pleasure only for the weekend. A little looking around near home may turn up an unsuspected stretch of whitewater. It doesn't need to be much —even as little as 25 yards will do. Toss the boat in after supper and practice ferrying, turning, and reversing. Really to sharpen your skills, hang a gate and practice the English Gate drill described in Chapter 10.

Or just plain fool around.

BASIC SAFETY CHECKLIST

No matter what sort of cruise you're planning, it should include the following basic considerations for safety. Observing them will allow you to concentrate on having a good time.

Use ALL the equipment required for any situation.

This means, for whitewater, lifejacket, helmet, spray-skirt, and flotation devices. If the water temperature is below 50° F.—and it usually is throughout the spring run-off season—wear a wet-suit.

Never run a river alone.

Always have at least one experienced companion in another boat along with you. If you dump and have to make a beeline for shore your companion can intercept your boat or paddle and nose it to shore.

Be sure that somebody else knows your plans.

There should always be someone alerted to send help to look for you if you don't return in a reasonable period of time.

Never run a river before you have scouted it thoroughly.

Remember the Saturday matinée when the hero and heroine are about to be swept over the waterfall? Wonder Dog may not be on the bankside just when you need him.

Never paddle in water you wouldn't want to swim in.

No matter how expert your Eskimo Roll, some day you may come detached from your boat and *have* to swim. (And of course if you can't swim well, you shouldn't be kayaking on the river at all.)

Know how to handle your boat after a Wet Exit.

If you have to make an exit, keep your boat upside down to minimize the amount of water it will ship. Then quickly get upstream of the overturned boat and guide it toward shore while hanging on to the *upstream* grabloop.

Never get downstream of a kayak filled with water—particularly if the current is carrying it toward a rock in the river, for the boat will hit like a ton of bricks.

Be sure you understand the phenomenon of rapidly moving water.

There is always more to contend with in swift current than what turbulence you may see on the surface. What are the signs of underwater obstructions? How will the water behave as it meets, and passes, them?

Don't be foolhardy about rapids beyond your ability.

Paddle in water that challenges your technical skill by all means, but don't hesitate to portage around a stretch that you feel you can't deal with safely and successfully.

HOW FAR, HOW FAST?

There is a tendency for newcomers to overestimate what is for them a comfortable paddling distance. After 12 miles and many tiring portages with their new canoe, a neighbor's marriage was in jeopardy. At Mile 8, after begging him to stop, his wife climbed out and waded ashore, leaving him muttering to himself as he paddled away with blistered hands.

In Class II water—moderate whitewater—expect to average about 4 to 5 miles per hour if you just paddle straight downriver and don't play around in eddies.

Most people find they are pleasantly tired after a couple of hours of whitewater paddling. There is a significant hazard in pressing on to exhaustion, for whitewater river running demands a certain amount of strength, quick thinking, and quick reflexes. When exhaustion saps your strength and dulls your responses, the possibility of an accident increases.

Flatwater paddling doesn't present the same potential danger from exhaustion. In sluggish current expect to average 3 miles per hour paddling at a comfortable rate.

GETTING TO/IN THE WATER

Each minute of planning beforehand will ensure hours' more pleasure on the water. Logistics is a part of any outing where thinking ahead really pays off after you have chosen your river and decided on the length of trip.

Put-in points

A put-in point should at the very least be a place with slack current along the riverbank. Getting into a kayak is tricky enough, and with the boat bouncing around it's that much harder. Obviously, then, a gentle bank is preferable for access and a stretch of flatwater is nice for a warm-up.

Be sure to ask permission of the landowner before trampling through his land or leaving cars parked about. Take care to park so as not to interfere with traffic if your put-in point is on a highway right-of-way.

Take-out points

For your take-out point choose a spot with little or no current—a wide stretch of the river with slack riverbank current or a riverbank eddy, for instance.

Again, a gentle, sloping riverbank is desirable. And observe all the basic courtesies in parking, etc.

Once out of the boats, be sure to haul them out of the water—even a slight current will cause a lightweight kayak to drift.

It is a good idea to mark take-out points or portages so these places can be seen from the water. When you're scouting the river beforehand, tie a piece of bright-colored plastic cloth to a tree branch that overhangs the water. This will alert paddlers and save a long walk back should they breeze merrily past the take-out area.

CAR-TOPPING

Getting your kayak to the river is really no problem. Put it on top of your car. Ingenuity manifests itself in car-topping, so don't be surprised to see up to six kayaks on one rooftop.

The basic equipment is minimal. You will need a roof-rack and preferably a pair of contoured cradles for each kayak. Buy plenty of weather-resistant rope—polypropylene or nylon work well. Mount the cradles on the rack so they support the first and last thirds of the kayak. Place the boat in the cradles and lash it securely to the rack. Use the grabloops at the bow and stern for attaching a line to each bumper for extra security should the rack ever work loose on your rooftop.

A roof rack and contoured cradles support a kayak in style. The bow and stern are tied down to the bumpers, elasticized cords secure the boat to the rack, and the paddle is fastened alongside the kayak. (R.F.G.)

Ideally your party should have a pair of cars, so one can be left at the take-out point at the end of the run.

If you have a choice of vehicles, station wagons or light pickup trucks are best. Car-top the boats to the put-in point, where you unload them. Then you and another driver take both vehicles to the take-out point; there you leave one, and both of you return back upstream in the other to the starting place. Leave the keys hidden carefully near each vehicle, so there's no chance they'll get lost if you or the other driver must wet-exit.

When the entire party has paddled to the take-out point, two drivers can use the downstream car to fetch the car left upstream and bring it back to the take-out point, where boats, gear, and people can be loaded for the drive home.

This seems at first glance to be the "fox-goose-and-grain" game we played as kids, but it's really a simple shuttle that leaves no one waiting by the roadside for his lift at the end of the run.

Only one car? Stash a bicycle near your take-out point and then later pedal back to pick up the car. Or you can hitchhike. Motorists are pretty good about picking up paddlers wearing lifejackets. Be sure to arrange the kayaks so that it is obvious what you have been doing as well as obvious that you do not expect the driver to take both you *and* your companions *and* your kayaks.

THE GROUP

Safety lies in numbers—that's why you never run a river alone.

When you're organizing a trip for more than two people, bear in mind that the perfect group is composed of a strong, experienced paddler (who can remember what it was like to be inexperienced) in the lead, a paddler with plenty of experience as the "sweep" at the rear, and in between all sorts of paddlers with a variety of skills. No member of any group should be unequal to the river's class, however, for this will lead only to his becoming humiliated, frustrated, and thoroughly miserable after repeated Wet Exits.

There is an established procedure used by any group to run a

All the ingredients for a successful outing: boats, paddles, safety equipment, and a group of enthusiastic kayakers of all ages. (L.C.C.)

stretch of rapids. The leader scouts the water ahead—from the bankside if necessary—and he then runs the stretch and waits for the rest of the group to come through.

If someone goes over and can't make a Roll up, the leader uses his discretion, either aiding the swimming paddler or retrieving the floating boat and/or the paddle.

The rest of the group runs the same stretch in descending order of competence: better first, newcomers to the sport last. They too hang about with the leader, waiting for any débris washing down.

And finally the sweep comes down. His function, in addition to any necessary assistance a situation requires, is to confirm that everybody and everything has gotten through.

WHAT TO TAKE ON A DAY TRIP

Right at the outset, take the basics for safety (in addition to cruising whitewater in company, *never* alone)—and this means being fully equipped with lifejackets, helmets, spray-skirts, and flotation bags for everyone in your party.

The next consideration: the fiberglass kayak is designed for performance, not cargo. If at all possible try *not* to stuff cargo in the ends of the kayak. The more weight you add there, the more you alter the intended performance characteristics of the boat. So use this space as a last resort against loss and try to secure gear, if possible, amidships.

Equipment and Clothing

A checklist is a great thing: imagine yourself 200 miles from home without your paddle! So think of what you'll need in addition to your party's safety gear.

Spare paddle? A take-apart paddle is a sensible solution. Tape the halves to the deck with duct tape. Use enough extra tape in the process to have enough for minor boat repairs, or throw the rest of the roll in one end of your kayak.

Dry clothes? It's always nice to get out of a wet, clammy paddling jacket into a nice dry one. If you're wearing a wet-suit, you'll be warm enough after you are done kayaking, but you may begin to feel as if you were wrinkling up like a prune; here a change of clothes is in order.

Waterproof bags come in the surplus-Army-Navy-store variety and the wilderness-outfitter-store variety. Into the bag of your choice go lunch, dry clothes, camera, and whatever else you think you really need. Secure the bag to the hipbrace by its shoulder strap, if it has one; if it doesn't, lash it with light rope. If for some reason you must stow it farther from you, stuff it ahead of your forward flotation bag or behind your stern flotation, remembering that the added weight will affect the trim, and therefore the handling, of your boat. Whichever method of stowing you use will keep you from losing your waterproof bag if you have to wet-exit.

A length of nylon or polypropylene line can also be tossed in— but in one end of the boat, not amidships, lest you become entangled with it in the event of a Wet Exit. Such a line can help no end in towing off a boat broadsided against a rock.

What else? Wet-suit, shoes, gloves—you might want to thumb

through a wilderness-outfitter catalogue: jackknife, sun glasses, waterproof matches, notebook and pencil, a river guidebook, canteen, snake-bite kit, water-purifying kit if you're going to be in waters of doubtful potability.

Food

The kayak is different from the canoe. What it gains in whitewater performance and safety, it loses in sociability and cargo space. The cookout stove, steak, cans of beans, etc., that can be easily stored in a canoe would burst the poor kayak. If you plan to eat on the riverbank en route, consider the dehydrated trail snacks that require no cooking, available at wilderness outfitters. Or pack your favorite high-energy, low-bulking fare.

Since most kayaking is done in cool weather and because you occasionally get an inadvertent mouthful of the river's water, thirst is rarely a significant problem. Kayaking, although it is strenuous, doesn't present the same dehydration problems common to cyclists and runners. A hip flask of an electrolyte replacement liquid should be a consideration, however. Remember what any endurance athlete has painfully learned: eat before you are hungry, drink before you are thirsty.

It is a good idea to plan your trip so you eat before you run fairly long or demanding rapids.

CAMPING

This is not intended to tell you how to camp but to alert you to the unique challenges you will face. We will have to assume that as far as camping goes you know what you're doing.

WHERE?

Campsite selection is best done before taking to the river. It's better to be conservative in spacing your pre-arranged campsites. Kayaking is a strenuous sport and you don't want to be miles from your next camp dog-tired with darkness settling in. If campsites cannot be pre-arranged, take a good one when you find it. There is no turning back in whitewater. A good guidebook and map are absolutely essential for camping.

CARGO

For better cargo carrying, swap the stern bag for a second bow bag, which is smaller, to give yourself more room just behind the cockpit.

For real camping you are dependent on the modern lightweight back-packing gear. The old-fashioned camping equipment of canvas and wood is too bulky and heavy. Today's tents and sleeping bags are both light and compact.

In addition to the items mentioned for day trips, consider: folding saw (not bulky axe or hatchet); knives, forks, spoons, pots, pans (collapsible, interlocking type), butane stove; extra underwear, socks, sneakers, rain gear, insect repellent, sun-tan lotion, chapstick, toothbrush, razor, soap, and toilet paper.

WILDERNESS WHITEWATER RIVER TOURING

The great rivers of North America—such as the Colorado, the Rogue, the Mackenzie, the Salmon, the Rio Grande, the Chattooga, the Cheat, and many others—provide the ultimate whitewater experience. A great deal of planning and expertise is necessary before setting out on one of these rivers. Civilization is generally a long way off and the paddler has to be able to mend a broken boat or a broken limb.

Because it is necessary to carry considerable supplies, many parties combine rafts and kayaks. The whale-like raft floats the party's gear and, if necessary, extra kayaks. The paddlers are then able to cope with the waters—often Class IV, Class V, and sometimes even Class VI—without the burden of cargo.

Running these great rivers is such a specialized topic that it is beyond the realm of this book. There are fine books on the subject that should be thoroughly studied as basic preparation by anyone even considering such a trip.

FLATWATER TOURING

The fiberglass kayak with its minimal draft is ideal for shallow-water cruising and exploring, and the maneuverable slalom type will wiggle its way through a dense swamp that would virtually immobilize a canoe or motorboat. For open-water paddling—lakes and wide rivers—the kayak's low profile means that it is little affected by the wind, which is the bane of open canoes.

You can get quite close to wildlife in a kayak if your approach is quiet. A little care in paddling will eliminate a lot of the splashing that sets birds to flight and turtles ducking for cover.

If you are interested in wildlife photography, hang the camera around your neck. Don't discard your spray-skirt and set the camera between your legs on the floor of the kayak, because the camera may get wet from water dripping off the paddle-shaft. By using the spray-skirt you can keep out marauding insects, too.

For extended flatwater cruising, comfort is a vital concern. Maintaining the braced position is cramping after several hours, and the wandering tendencies of the slalom design can be frustrating.

As mentioned before, cargo-carrying capacity is severely limited and improper loading will negatively affect the kayak's performance.

When paddling in flatwater occasionally dip each hand into the water. The water will act as a lubricant between the paddle-shaft and the palm of the hand, preventing blisters.

This C–2 touring model features a special center hatch for storing cargo. The bow and stern ends are curved upward to emulate the lines of the classic Canadien canoe. (OLD TOWN CANOE COMPANY)

8 *Whitewater Racing*

[J . E .]

RACING sharpens the serious kayaker's skills and makes him the supreme master of his boat. It provides the mental stimulation so necessary for a commitment to excellence. Finally, it fosters a quality and depth of comradeship unknown to many milder endeavors: the friends you make are forever.

To be truthful about it, kayaking looks far more dangerous than it really is. Statistically, kayaking is far less risky than bicycling. Kayak racing—done properly, using good common water-sense and safety equipment—is one of the safest of sports.

There are many fine opportunities for racing in the United States and Canada. The national and state whitewater clubs listed in the Appendix will supply information about major races, cruising, and other competitive and recreational aspects of whitewater kayaking and canoeing.

WORLD COMPETITION

The International Canoe Federation, the world-wide governing body with headquarters in Europe, recognizes several broad categories of closed-deck canoe and kayak competitions, including whitewater slalom and wildwater races. The first appearance of whitewater slalom as an Olympic event was in 1972 at Munich; until then only flatwater canoeing and kayaking were included in the Games.

In both whitewater slalom and wildwater racing the ICF recognizes five classes within the scope of this book: *K–1* (man in a kayak); *K–1W* (woman in a kayak); *C–1* (man in a closed-deck canoe); *C–2* (two men in a closed-deck canoe); and *C–2M* (man and woman in a closed-deck canoe).

The ICF also allows team races in each class in both slalom and wildwater. A team race consists of three boats of the same class representing the same club or country.

NORTH AMERICAN RACING

National championships in both Canada and the United States in the various classes are not always held in the same place each year. The national kayaking championships for both men and women in recent years were in Connecticut, California, Washington and Colorado. In Canada, national championships have been held to date in the provinces of Quebec, Ontario, British Columbia and Alberta.

New competitions are cropping up so fast that a listing here would be inadequate and obsolete within a season. For the latest information you should write to your national association—ACA, AWA or CCA—with a self-addressed, postage-paid return envelope.

Marathons and Other Specialties

Marathon racing, particularly popular in the Middle West, usually involves mostly open canoes that are specially designed for speed. Marathons rarely are run through extensive rapids.

If your preference leans toward the open canoe, the ACA has sanctioned national championships in open-canoe racing in both whitewater slalom and wildwater. These championships originated in Maine, where running rapids in an open canoe is a popular pastime.

One of the most enjoyable aspects of kayaking is its spontaneity. For the past several years, for example, a group of enthusiasts from the Concord–Carlisle High School in Massachusetts has sponsored an informal kayak race on Thoreau's Concord River in early November. A raw, cold, rainy day is almost guaranteed, but this doesn't dampen anyone's spirits.

Those who wish to combine kayaking and skiing can do so. The annual Sugarloaf Canoe-Ski weekend, held in Maine each April, combines a ski race with a paddle down a nearby rapids. And those who wish to combine kayaking, skiing *and* bicycling had a golden opportunity at Lake Tahoe in California where, in the spring of 1974, a 15-mile Boards, Bikes and Boats race was held.

There is such a broad spectrum of possibilities for racing that almost everyone's needs and desires can be met. Nevertheless, if yours isn't, then go ahead and organize your own race (see Chapter 9).

A Code for the Racer

Whitewater racing is marvelously rewarding, thanks in part to its prevailing spirit of good fellowship and fair play. To make sure that this spirit is not eroded as the competitions grow, we propose the following code for racers.

Be realistic about your degree of competence. There are increasing numbers of boaters anxious to race who have not yet perfected the Eskimo Roll, the most reliable way to get out of trouble. The answer to this problem rests largely in the hands of the race officials, who will determine that only competent kayakers may enter events that tax their skills. The kayaker has an obligation not to oversell his or her abilities.

Never enter a race without studying the course beforehand. Skill seldom compensates for bad judgment arising from ignorance of where obstacles lie. So get out to the river where the race will be run and study its haystacks, rollers, eddies and chutes. Walk along its banks, spotting obstructions that lurk underwater.

Race with all the equipment necessary for safety. You owe it to yourself and everybody else to ensure that a mishap does not become a full-fledged emergency because you, and your boat, are not properly outfitted. This means life-jacket, helmet, and wet-suit if it is indicated, for you; grab-loops and flotation bags for your boat. To protect yourself against chill, use pogies or gloves and have warm clothing handy at the end of your run.

Bring your own equipment for every race. Borrowing equipment is poor form indeed, aside from being a nuisance. Bring an extra paddle, if possible. Have your name on each piece of your gear.

Follow the rules of any competition your enter. Race organizers have good reasons for the regulations they make. Therefore don't ask for special dispensation or consideration. Send your entry form in on time—completely filled out and with the correct entry fee attached. On race day, be patient with race organizers and be alert for chances to be helpful. Protest only for the most valid reasons.

Be gracious, win or lose. The true sportsman will congratulate the winner, and will never be a sore loser. (And a thank-you note to the committee after the race will certainly be appreciated!)

Whitewater Slalom

The very first Olympic whitewater slalom was held in 1972 near Munich, where 38,000 people stood tensely by the edge of the Olympic course at the Eis Kanal. The race so fascinated the general public that in the following year the American Broadcasting Company filmed the kayak segment of the World Whitewater Championships from Muota, Switzerland, for their "Wide World of Sports" program, which was shown on nationwide television. Truly, whitewater kayak racing had caught the fancy of the sporting world.

"Fishpole" gates mark the course in this beginners' slalom race. (L.C.C.)

Precious few racers will ever be fortunate enough to compete in an Olympic or World Championship experience with the eyes of world television upon them. But what may begin as a simple desire to sneak one's kayak between two rocks could develop into a taste for slalom or wildwater racing—and who knows where that may lead?

THE ANATOMY OF SLALOM

Whitewater slalom consists of paddling, in the fastest possible time, a stretch of challenging rapids whose demands have been increased tenfold by the introduction of additional, and artificial, obstacles. These obstacles are the gates—wooden poles dangling from a cross-bar suspended over a stretch of highly turbulent water not more than 800 meters long.

There is no such thing as a standard championship slalom course like the 100-yard hurdles in track-and-field events. Rather, each slalom is laid out to create a unique series of challenges posed by the natural obstacles in the rapids in concert with the placing of the gates. Almost any number of gates will do, ranging from 12 or 15 in smaller local races to the 30 gates at most international competitions. The racer must go through each gate in the proper order (each is numbered), and in the proper direction (some must be negotiated upstream or backward).

Paddlers race separately against the clock, each trying for the least amount of time—and the least number of penalties for touching a gate or failing to follow the course correctly. The racer is given two runs on the course; the better run is the one that counts. The score is the total number of seconds taken to complete the course, plus the number of penalty points accrued, added in seconds.

Penalty Points

If you touch the inside face of a pole while negotiating a gate correctly 10 points (seconds) are added to your total time. Add another 10 points if you hit both poles on the inside. Suppose you get swept downstream, miss a gate entirely and never get back to do it: 50 points added. If you manage to get close enough to touch the gate from the outside but then don't go through it: 50 points added.

If you capsize as you go through a gate: 50 points. If you get confused and take a gate in the wrong direction: 50 points. If you touch a gate from the outside but still manage to get through it: only 20 points.

There are some other fine distinctions in the judging of gates, but

Swept too close to the gate to turn in time, a racer hits both poles broadside. This will mean a 20-point penalty, if the racer can recover and get his body between the gate poles; otherwise, 50 points if he misses the gate entirely. (KOLIVAS PHOTO)

these will do as a starter. The thing to remember is to make your boat go through the gates properly *without touching.*

The Three Gates

For slalom you must think in terms of three major man-made obstacles: (1) the downstream gate; (2) the upstream gate; and (3) the reverse gate.

THE DOWNSTREAM GATE

This is the most common gate in whitewater slalom. In most situations the downstream gate should be taken at full speed, without interrupting your stroke, and at an angle that will line up your boat for getting quickly to the *next* gate.

Common mistakes:

Hitting a pole with the paddle as you stroke through the gate.

Not being lined up properly before you go through the gate.

Allowing your stern to touch a pole as you leave the gate.

Looking back as you go through the gate to see if you have cleared it. (It is too late for you to do anything at that point, and it will break your concentration on the next gate.)

THE UPSTREAM GATE

This gate often lurks behind rocks and in eddies.

The idea is to go down beside the gate, turn around, and then come back up through it as fast as possible. This calls for unusually accurate depth perception as your boat closes in on the gate. As you make your swing into position (probably using a Sweep stroke or a Duffek) your bow should never be more than an inch or two from the pole closer to you and around which you must pivot. Then, angle your boat so you'll be lined up correctly to make a minimum arc toward the next gate as you drive hard with Forward strokes through the upstream gate. An upstream gate negotiated in 5 seconds or less can be considered a competent piece of work.

Common mistakes:

Swinging too far below the gate into the eddy. (The current will tend to move you farther downstream than you expect.)

Misjudging the eddy current and thus making an outside (or inside) touch on a pole as you swing into and through the gate. (Study the current and the eddy carefully beforehand.)

Swinging out too far upstream after clearing the gate.

THE REVERSE GATE

This one attracts the most penalties in whitewater slalom, mostly because it is the gate that is practiced the least. A reverse gate is just like a downstream gate except for one thing: your boat must go through it *backward.* (Only rarely will there be a reverse gate that must be negotiated upstream.)

First, in approaching a reverse gate keep your eye constantly on the pole that will be the nearer one to you as you pass through the gate, and never take your eye off that pole.

Second, spin your boat around directly in front of the gate. Don't waste valuable seconds by turning too soon. Drive hard with strong Back strokes at an angle that will place you in the proper position for the next gate.

Third, begin to turn toward the next gate *immediately* after your bow clears the pole.

Common mistakes:

Not looking at the gate soon enough as you approach it.

Not keeping your eye on the pole constantly as you turn in front of the gate.

Turning before the gate either too early or too late.

Floating through, rather than powering your way through, the gate.

Dropping below the gate too far (more than 1 inch) after the bow is clear.

"Pivotitis"—looking first over one shoulder, then over the other shoulder as you approach the gate. (If you are closing in properly on the nearer pole, you automatically know exactly how far away you are from the other one.)

Not twisting your body around enough so that *both* eyes can concentrate on the pole.

Putting It All Together

MEMORIZING THE COURSE

From a close study of the course, preferably from both riverbanks, you must get the entire route firmly planted in your mind. Ideally it is best to arrive at the race site a day or two in advance to get settled, but short of that you should plan to get out early on the morning of the race to acquaint yourself with the water conditions and all details of the course.

By this intensive study you should develop a clear-cut program of attack and get it firmly in mind. Take along a notebook and a pencil. Watch carefully to see how the good boaters do it if free practice is allowed on the course ahead of time. Those who have difficulty remembering a whole course might try clumping the gates in their minds. Think of several gates as a unit, and go over in your mind how you plan to tackle them.

THE DECISIONS INVOLVED

At each gate you must make three decisions:

1. At what angle should I approach so I get the fastest line on to the next gate?

2. Exactly where will I place my paddle the very moment I am clear of the gate?

3. If something goes wrong, can I duck into the nearest piece of friendly water and make a second attempt at the gate? (If the rules allow this, it is better to use an extra 15 seconds than to settle for the ignominy of a permanent 50-point penalty for missing the gate altogether.)

THE WARM-UP

Most people simply don't warm up enough before the race itself. A good warm-up prepares the body for the large load it will soon be

Study the entire course before a race to get the route firmly in mind. These competitors are checking out a slalom course the day before a water release. (L.C.C.)

asked to bear and—even more important—it helps to reduce nervous tension. If the race is held in the morning, you should get up at least five hours before your run to make sure that you are operating on all cylinders by race time.

Always remember that a full stomach prevents good breathing, so don't eat anything for at least a couple of hours before the race.

You should paddle hard for 10 minutes somewhere upstream of the start, out of the way. If this is impossible, jog and sprint along a nearby path or road, and do some limbering-up and stretching exercises. Your pulse-rate should be up around 100, and you should have developed a pretty good sweat just before the countdown.

THE START

Shake your arms, shoulders and wrists to loosen them. Relax your trunk muscles and take a few deep breaths to fill your lungs with oxygen. Make a final check of your spray-skirt. Listen carefully to the cadence of the countdown for other racers, so you can anticipate the split second when "Go" is called for your boat.

At the start a standing boat must be brought into motion, and to overcome inertia and accelerate to top racing speed requires considerable strength. Also at the start, keep your boat pointed a few degrees inside of the direction line you wish to follow so your first maximum-power Forward stroke can be employed without the immediate necessity of making a correcting stroke.

When the start is electronic, *if it is permissible* back off a bit to try to get one or two strokes in so your boat will be well underway before the electric eye is triggered.

IT'S A RACE

You can waste much of the advantage gained from good gate technique if you loaf between gates. Just keep in mind that an American National Slalom title was lost not too many years ago by 0.6 second! Most gates are about 20 yards apart, so you have a chance to gain a little between gates if you hustle.

After the last gate is behind you, really pour it on and *sprint* not just to the finish line, but to a point at least one full boat-length beyond. This will guarantee that your boat crosses the real finish line in the fastest possible way.

Between Runs

After your run get into dry clothes as soon as possible. Get comfortable, but don't eat anything right away—a little honey, a sweetened drink, or a small candy bar or an orange will do. Stay out of the sun: both sun and wet clothes sap energy. When the time comes for your second run be sure to warm up as thoroughly as you did for your first run.

And good luck!

The Wildwater Race

Basically a wildwater race consists of a start somewhere upriver with a finish line anywhere from 2 to 15 miles or more downriver. No penalty points are involved and the winner is the racer with the shortest elapsed time between start and finish. Compared to slalom, which rarely exceeds 4 minutes, a wildwater race will take anywhere from 9 to 30 minutes or more depending upon the length of the course. The trick is to find the swiftest route through the rapids.

THE FASTEST ROUTE

Familiarity with the course is not only helpful technically, but gives the racer a great psychological boost. Every rock in the river, every new view around the bend, should be a familiar, beckoning sight.

In a wildwater race, "full speed ahead" is the basic strategy for all racers. (KLEPPER-WERKE PHOTO)

Running the course several times at the same water level at which the race will be conducted, and experimenting with different routes, will add the knowledge necessary for winning.

Avoid eddies that will catch your bow and spin you around, and be wary of rollers and stoppers that slow your forward movement. Avoid "bottom drag"—an insidious braking action which measurably slows your boat when the water is too shallow.

Once the fastest route has been determined, go over each part of it in your mind just as carefully as you would the gates of a slalom. Develop a mental picture of it section by section.

THE START

Most wildwater starts are done singly with 1-minute or 2-minute intervals between boaters. If this is the case, simply leap off that starting line as fast as possible and do everything in your power to close the gap between you and the boater who took off ahead of you.

In the case of a multiple start (two or three boats at a time) when the field is particularly large, it is important to sprint out in front immediately and stay there. Let the rest of the pack jockey for position behind you.

OVERTAKING

If you catch up to a boater it is legal (except for flatwater racing) to ride his wake—assuming that he takes what you *know* to be the fastest route! Just being right on his tail may make him nervous, will make it easier for you to paddle, and can help you to pace yourself.

If you overtake another boater and are ready to pass him, he must give way to allow you room to pass. Simply yell "Track!" as in skiing, and he is obliged to move over.

SPLITS

Splits can be a handy way of keeping track of your speed in comparison with other boaters in a wildwater race. You need a confed-

---

Good Samaritans

Since much wildwater racing involves stretches of rapids often in a canyon or valley away from civilization, any racer who sees another boater in trouble and in need of help must stop, discontinue racing immediately and go to his aid. Failure to do so can mean disqualification forever. Let's face it, human life is more important than a piece of blue ribbon; and besides, just put yourself in his wet-suit for a moment. You'll be glad you helped. You can always race another day.

---

erate with a stopwatch, a bicycle or car, and a good working knowledge of the backroads and paths near the river.

For example, your friend knows that the person you would like to beat is 2 minutes ahead of you in the starting order. The split-taker will station himself at some mutually agreed upon place down from the start (bridges are always handy). He'll start his stopwatch as your adversary goes by. If you haven't gained on him, then you should also pass by when the split-taker's stopwatch reaches the 2-minute mark. If you appear in 1 minute and 40 seconds, this means that you have gained 20 seconds on your opponent. The message will be shouted to you loud and clear by your friend on the bridge, and welcome news it is. And if you have fallen behind, the information thus relayed to you should give you renewed determination to step up the pace.

THE FINISH

As soon as the finish line comes into sight is the time for an all-out sprint. No need to conserve energy or to pace yourself any longer.

Just keep constantly in mind that some races are lost by a fraction of a second. At the World Championships in 1973 the difference between a bronze and a silver medal in wildwater K–1 was only 0.8 second over a 17-minute course.

As in slalom, always paddle *through* the finish line, not simply *to* it. Then paddle around a bit to "warm down" until your pulse rate is back to 100 or less. Don't drink or eat anything for at least half an hour after the race.

9 The Race Organizer's Checklist
[J . E .]

THE POPULARITY of whitewater competition is growing so fast that race organization requires efficiency and long-range planning. Running a race can be a source of enormous pride and satisfaction at seeing an event unfold smoothly, or it can turn into an endurance contest. By following a reasonably strict timetable spread over several months, it is possible not only to organize a race successfully but to enjoy it as well. The better the preliminary work behind the scenes before race day, the better the race turns out.

SIX MONTHS BEFORE THE RACE

Where/When/Who

Choose the site, the time of the race, and the kind of race you want—slalom, wildwater, or possibly both. Obtain permission of the landowners on each side of the river where you propose to hold the events. Next, decide what kind of race it should be: experts only, beginners, or an all-comers race open to anyone. Determine what classes to offer. The ICF recognizes K–1, K–1W, C–1, C–2, and C–2M; you may want to add divisions for junior, senior, beginner, intermediate and expert boaters. Decide the number of entries you can safely handle in terms of available manpower, camping, parking and toilet facilities, etc.

Publicity

After the basics have been decided, make sure the race gets listed in *Canoe* (the American Canoe Association magazine) and in the annual *Whitewater Racing Program* so people will learn about the race. Since most publications go to press months in advance of their cover date, be sure to check on the deadlines for getting your information to the editors.

At the same time, ask the American Canoe Association for sanction. Write for permission to hold the race, listing the date, location, kind of race, any limitations, and the name and address of the person who has been designated to provide information.

THREE MONTHS BEFORE THE RACE

Paperwork

Entry forms for a well-run race should be mailed out a month to six weeks before the race date. Be sure to allow for the amount of time it will take to prepare and print the forms and mail them out. Entry forms should include the following: time, place, date, starting time; description of the course, race categories, water conditions; liability release; entry fee and deadlines; and an address to which entries should be sent.

It is helpful, but not necessary, to mention whether there will be a shuttle service or food for sale, and to give the addresses of conveniently located motels and campgrounds in the race area.

Manpower

Assign one person as the race registrar to keep track of all the entrants and whether or not they've paid the entry fee, so at any time he can report how many racers have entered and who is racing in what class. The registrar's duties last until race day is over, and are linked closely with those of several other committees.

All told you should line up 50 percent more manpower than you think you'll need (most of your help will be volunteers, and therefore many well-meant promises might not be kept at the last minute). For a slalom race the following positions need to be filled: registrar, timers, scorers, recorders, gate judges, safety crew, gate-adjustment crews, protest committee, results coordinator, press officer, communications crew and starters.

For wildwater all these positions need to be filled except, of course, the gate judges and gate-adjustment crews needed for slalom races.

Numbering/Amenities/Water Level

The race registrar can also distribute and collect numbered racing bibs on race day. Bibs are available from ski areas and outing clubs, canoe companies and some sports-clothing outfitters. Paper bibs, which are beginning to replace the traditional cloth ones, will hold up well enough in whitewater to last a weekend, and make a nice souvenir of the race to take home.

Occasionally one will see a large white decal pasted on the deck of the boat with the racer's number written on the decal. This system works fine unless two racers want to use the same boat—in which case the first decal must be removed and a new decal applied in its place.

Check with groups that might want to set up food concessions. And be sure to inform local police about the race and alert them to any possible traffic problems.

If there is a dam upstream of the race site, investigate the possibility of having a water release timed for your race.

Equipment

Start collecting all the needed equipment several months in advance of a race—including gates, wire, rope, string, communications materials, clipboards, scoreboards, typewriter and safety gear.

A Slalom Primer

THE COURSE

A good slalom course should take advantage of the natural obstacles in the rapids yet should be laid out so that an expert racer can make a smooth and penalty-free run. Whenever possible there should be as many turn-outs (or break-outs, as the British say) to the right as to the left, and the course should include several upstream gates and reverse gates. One North American K–1 champion gives this additional advice for designing a slalom course: "Rarely a reverse gate first, or last, or back-to-back."

A full-blown slalom of 30 gates will meet international specifications, but for most competitions 12 to 20 gates will do nicely. Don't be too ambitious: any more than that will overtax many paddlers' stamina, and problems of communications will begin to multiply for the race committee.

THE SLALOM GATE

A slalom gate consists of a wooden crosspiece with a pole dangling from each end. A small board hangs from the middle of the crosspiece to display the gate number. The gate hangs from a wire that has been stretched across the river high enough to let each dangling pole just clear the surface of the water.

The simplest form of gate has the poles permanently attached to the crosspiece, with the entire gate capable of being raised or lowered by adjusting the suspension wire over the stream. This rudimentary gate is not really satisfactory, however, because one pole should hang higher than the other if the rapids below are uneven. It is important in a race that *each pole,* regardless of its length, hang just clear of the water.

GATE COMPONENTS

Crosspiece boards should be 6 or 7 feet long to allow for adequate spacing of the poles. According to ICF regulations, the width of the gate must be at least 1.2 meters (about 4 feet) and no more than 3.5 meters (just over 11 feet). At most slalom races, the gates are between 4 and 5 feet wide. Decide on the width of your gate and space 2 metal screw-eyes that distance apart, equidistant from the ends of the crosspiece. Also at the ends of the crosspiece, attach shower-curtain rings through which a wire can be threaded when stringing gates across a river.

Two *poles* are needed for each gate. Paint one pole in alternating bands of white and green, the other in white and red. When you string the gate over the river, the green-striped pole will be on the paddler's right as he goes through the gate, with the red-and-white pole on his left.

A *gate-number board* about 15 inches square hangs from the crosspiece between the poles to identify each gate. Paint both sides of the board yellow, with the gate number in black; add a diagonal red stripe on the backside of the board in the international sign for "no entry," so the racer knows which direction to approach it from. If the gate is a reverse or team gate, an additional "R" or "T" board must hang beside the number board.

STRINGING A GATE

For the uninitiated, gate-stringing seems quite a puzzle, but basically the set-up is similar to that of a clothesline on pulleys, stretching between a porch and a garage. Just as you haul clothes toward you by pulling on the line, gate-stringers move a gate from one side of the river to the other on a lead line.

The gate itself hangs from a wire; the gate's position is controlled by separate lines attached to the ends of the crosspiece. Another set of lines holds the poles to the crosspiece; these lines should be run from both poles to the same shore, so that individual poles can be adjusted easily from only one side of the river.

While a gate crew holds the lines that regulate the height of each pole, a crew on the other side of the river will pull this gate into position over the water. (L.C.C.)

ON RACE DAY

Safety

No matter what sort of waiver a racer may sign to release the organizing committee from liability for damage suffered during a race, the organizers are morally responsible to some degree for every boater's safety. Let's face it—there are increasing numbers of boaters eager to race before they've learned how to handle themselves in an emergency, much less to come to the aid of anyone else.

PREVENTIVE MEASURES

The most important preventive measure is simple: *make sure each boater's ability is equal to the difficulty of the water.* A beginners' race should always be held in easy water. If you're holding a race in difficult water, pre-screen the entrants and allow only qualified boaters in the race.

Another precautionary measure is holding a boat inspection before the race, not so much to see that the boats are of legal length and width, as to make sure they have ample flotation and a grabloop in both bow and stern for controlling the boat and towing it to shore after a capsize.

I vividly recall the Mascoma River Slalom of 1969 which took place under flood conditions. As the chief official, I allowed only the best-qualified 13 out of 50 entrants to race in that dangerous water. Some people were angry that day, but I preferred that they be disappointed rather than injured.

RESCUE

The best rescue of course is self-rescue, and for that, nothing quite compares with a reliable Eskimo Roll.

The trouble comes with racers who have not perfected the Roll. For them, a variety of arrangements for rescue from shore have been developed over the years.

A very effective measure is to ask at least *two boaters* to wait in their boats at the finish line while a third completes the course.

A rescuer on shore throws an innertube and line to a capsized boater. The kayaker has remembered to hang on to her boat and paddle. (L.C.C.)

This makes it easy to pick up paddles that come floating through, and to nudge a capsized boat toward shore.

Skin divers can be a great help—if they are familiar with the dynamics of rapidly moving water.

One of the most controversial provisions for rescue is a *line* with some kind of knob or knot attached to the end of it. Capsized racers have been hit on the head when the thrower was too accurate, or have become entangled in the rope. In addition, the knot or knob is usually hard to see in the rapids. It is much better to attach an inflated automobile innertube to the end of the line.

Communications

Effective communications are the key to a successful slalom. You need some means of knowing what's going on at the starting point, at a command post part way down the course, at the primary gate-checking stations, and at the finish line. At Olympic trials or major ICF races there is a gate-checker with a portable telephone reporting to the command post the penalties at every gate as they hap-

Gate judges with walkie-talkies stand near their assigned gate, ready to record and report penalties as they occur. (L.C.C.)

pen. However, at less luxurious competitions, one telephone often will have to cover at least five gates, with the other gate judges signaling the penalties to the telephone operator.

Walkie-talkies also make an efficient communications system. Of course you'll make sure that the sets are powerful enough to cover the length of the course.

Scoring

Scores must be posted promptly. The Dartmouth instant-scoring system, devised by Sandy Campbell, a member of the 1972 Olympic team, is a good one for either telephones or walkie-talkies.

From the race starter, the recorder at the command post gets the name, class and run-number of the racer about to depart. The recorder writes this information on an individual score sheet on a clipboard to which a stopwatch is attached. Over the walkie-talkie the recorder hears the starter give the racer the countdown, and starts his stopwatch as the racer begins. As the racer takes each gate, the gate judge reports any penalties over a walkie-talkie. The recorder follows the racer through the course, noting penalties as they are incurred, and he clicks the stopwatch when he hears the finish-line judge report that the boat has crossed the line. The recorder then hands over his stopwatch and score sheet to a scorer, who puts the results on the board for all to see.

Timing a Wildwater Race

In wildwater kayak racing, the most important single item, aside from safety, is *timing*. Make sure the timers are at the finish line when the first racer arrives. Synchronize your watches before the race begins so that the finish-line timers don't have to appear at the start at all.

Timers at the finish line need to have cool heads and keen eyes, because sometimes boats will cross the finish in a wild sprint and closely bunched, and it may be hard to see the race numbers.

A full finish-line crew should include one person who does nothing but read off the exact time, down to the second, as a given boat crosses the line. To verify his time-keeping, he should have at least one assistant with a back-up stopwatch. In addition there should be two recorders ready to write down the racer's number and/or name and his time as he crosses the finish line. The cards can then be arranged according to time and class so the results can be posted immediately after the race.

AFTER THE RACE

JUDGE AND JURY

In the event of a close call, a gate judge must have written down what happened, in case the race jury asks him to testify to decide a protest. All protests should be submitted by a team captain in writing immediately after the posting of scores. The jury's decision is final.

The boater himself is probably the poorest judge of all as to whether he touched a pole or not: he simply is not able to see the entire length of his boat on both sides simultaneously.

AWARDS

Decide well ahead of time what kind of awards you will give and be sure they are on hand the day of the race. There is nothing like trophies to stimulate interest and enthusiasm among inexperienced racers. Utilitarian-minded race organizers sometimes offer paddles for awards, or real mugs that can be used. I've seen pewter candlesticks given, and a nice leather briefcase was the prize for placing tenth in the K–1 class at Merano, Italy, one year.

An awards ceremony should be held immediately after a race. Here, an official presents medals to the top three competitors in the Colorado Cup races. (L.C.C.)

No matter what the awards are—mugs, cups, ribbons, or whatever—the important thing is for the awards ceremony to take place immediately following the race.

DEALING WITH THE PRESS

When dealing with the press, remember that the Fourth Estate has the last word as well as the first word, and, at its discretion, no word at all. However, many sportswriters welcome the chance to report such a refreshingly different event as a kayak race.

Good press relations are important, and detailing a couple of people to act as a publicity committee can help. The committee should send out a *factual* news release to local and regional papers before the event. Committee members should be on hand at the race to escort reporters, if necessary, and to supply them with facts about the events and information about the competitors, plus any real human-interest angles. A copy of the race results should be placed in each reporter's hands pronto.

In addition, send all race results to the American Canoe Association and to kayaking magazines.

10 *Tips on Training*
[J . E .]

WHITEWATER RACING demands total body performance. It also calls for stamina as well as strength, varying from a maximum output of effort for not more than 5 minutes in a slalom run, to 30 minutes or more in a wildwater race. If your body is conditioned to putting out concentrated, sustained effort for the required period of time, you will be able to focus on the immediate obstacles of the race and how to deal with them.

HOW FIT ARE YOU?

If you wish to take up racing seriously, you should step on the scales and then take an objective look at yourself in the mirror. What kind of shape are you in *now?* After getting medical clearance, see how far you can jog and run in 12 minutes. According to Dr. Kenneth Cooper's book *Aerobics,* an average active person can do up to 1.75 miles in 12 minutes, while a gold-medal-category athlete can cover 2.25 miles or more.

After you have established your current physical-fitness category, you can lay out a program for working up to your potential. You should have your doctor's permission to train, and you should warm up thoroughly before each workout. Figure on a period of at least 6 months before expecting any measurable improvement, and try to work out at least 5 days each week.

BUILDING STAMINA

Any or all of the following exercises will increase your stamina. If you can't do them for the prescribed length of time, simply do them for as long as you can, and gradually work up. And if these exercises are too easy for you, you're only cheating yourself unless you set your sights higher.

INTERVAL TRAINING

When water is available, get into your boat and try 50 rapid maximum-effort Forward strokes followed by a 10-second rest. Repeat this exercise six times or more. On land, run six 200-yard sprints, keeping track of your time. Try to lower your time with each sprint.

TEMPO TRAINING

Paddle at full racing speed for 20 percent of the length of time it takes to run a race. If you are training for slalom, try paddling all-out for 1 minute; for wildwater, paddle all-out for 2½ to 3 minutes, once for each quarter of the race. Repeat about five times. If you don't have access to water, run six consecutive ½-mile stretches in not more than 3 minutes each, taking a 1-minute rest between each ½ mile.

DISTANCE TRAINING

Ideally, this involves prolonged paddling for 30 minutes to an hour at racing speed against a stopwatch. Try to increase the distance you cover from week to week. If you can't get to water, jog or run for at least an hour non-stop.

BUILDING STRENGH

Strength is really nothing more than the power your body has available to accomplish a particular task. Stamina and strength go hand in hand as essential ingredients for good physical fitness. Do these exercises every day if you want to, or every other day. The

Building strength can start with simple exercises done regularly—push-ups, sit-ups, chin-ups. (R.R.A.)

important thing is to establish a definite routine and keep at it until it becomes a regular part of your life.

CHIN-UPS

How many you can do at a clip will depend on your body weight and frame, but if you are not physically out of proportion you should aim for two groups of 25 each in a period of a couple of minutes. Chin-ups develop the muscles in the forearm and the biceps.

PUSH-UPS

Push-ups work wonders to develop the triceps as well as the forearm. Aim for three groups of 40 push-ups in a couple of minutes.

SIT-UPS

Do three groups of 20 sit-ups in a couple of minutes. Hold your hands behind your head and your body rigid at a 45-degree angle for 20 seconds afterward, until those abdominal muscles really begin to shout for relief.

CIRCUIT EXERCISES

I recommend a neat six-station circuit exercise that requires only a barbell and weights, a 1-inch-diameter wooden dowel, and about 5 feet of rope. Complete the "circuit" three times in a row, allowing about 5 minutes for rest between each station.

1.   With a 10-pound weight held behind your head, do 20 *sit-ups*.
2.   Lying on your back with weights equal to two-thirds of your

body weight attached to the barbell, *bench-press* the barbell 10 times.

3.   Standing with a quarter of your body weight attached to the barbell and with your arms at your sides, palms out, raise the barbell to your chin, then lower it back to waist level; do this *curl* 10 times.

4.   Standing with a quarter of your body weight on the barbell and with your hands at your sides, palms in, raise the barbell to your chin with elbows high, then lower it; do this *upright row* 10 times.

5.   Sit with your forearms resting on top of your thighs, wrists extending just beyond kneecaps and palms facing out: *wrist-curl* the barbell up as high as you can until your forearms leave your thighs, 50 times.

6.   Stand with your arms fully extended in front of you, grabbing the dowel with both hands. Roll the dowel up, turning it so that a rope attached to the dowel will gradually lift a 10-pound weight tied to the other end of the rope; do this *roll* 10 times.

Race Training

Although there are many different kinds of kayak races, luckily training will cover all of them. Also, there is much overlap in technique from one kind of racing to another. The following exercises will help you train for almost any kind of race.

POOL TRAINING

There are municipal or private indoor pools in most communities of any size. The local kayak club can usually organize pool sessions by arrangement with public or private owners.

Pool training offers several advantages. The space-limits make coaching easier, and there is guaranteed lighting for the use of visual aids. The trick is to devise basic training techniques that call for very little water space but at the same time simulate outdoor conditions.

The roll

Above all, that pool water is warm! Those trying to conquer the Eskimo Roll on their weak side will find this a great help. You can make a game of it. Anyone can learn to roll using a paddle—eventually—but how about with a pair of ping-pong paddles, or better yet, using hands only?

Stunt men will be interested in seeing how many rolls they can do in 60 seconds. A competent roller in reasonably good physical condition should be able to complete up to 20 rolls in a minute. (The first time you try it, though, you'll believe that it is the longest minute of your life.)

The English Gate

The English Gate—developed in England, where it's called the "Wiggle Test"—is a complicated, back-and-forth, in-and-out maneuver to add flavor to flatwater, all around and through a single gate without touching a pole. It is particularly effective training for slalom and helps develop the quick, precise movements you need for wildwater racing.

First, pass through the gate in a forward direction three times.

Strenuous training exercises include the English Gate, a sequence of maneuvers around a single gate, performed at full speed. (L.C.C.)

Next, back your kayak down the outside of a pole, roll, then go forward through the gate and repeat the process on the other side. In the third phase, move again down the outside of a pole, pivot, and then go backward through the gate. Once through, pivot again and go backward through the gate. For the final phase, move forward past the outside of a pole, roll, then go backward through the gate and repeat the process on the other side.

The English Gate should be done flat-out at full speed. The occasional weekend racer really ought to complete an English Gate in 80 or 90 seconds; a U.S. Team prospect, in 60 to 70 seconds.

THE RACK

A rack consists of two wooden 2 × 4's connected by wooden cross-pieces like a ladder, with a molded kayak seat set in the middle. Attach the rack firmly to the side of the pool so that it projects directly out into the water, and support it from below so that it won't move. Place a full-length mirror in front of the kayak seat so that a boater can see his own strokes.

Using a stopwatch, take a stroke a second, and paddle in the rack for 5 minutes without once breaking rhythm. This exercise begins to simulate the physical strain that a boater experiences during a 20- or 25-gate slalom. You can vary the 5-minute time limit for interval and tempo training.

Don't try the rack with a full-bladed paddle: it has too much water resistance. Take an old paddle and shave the blades to about 3 inches wide.

Pool Games

THE CHASE

A three-man chase lasting for 5 minutes straight adds zest to any practice. At top speed, the paddler in Boat No. 1 leads the other boats on an unpredictable route for 5 minutes, through and around 4 or 5 gates that have been strung across the pool; he can also include an occasional Eskimo Roll. The object of the chase is for the lead boat to gain enough on his followers to approach and touch Boat No. 3 from the rear. All gates must be negotiated without touching the poles.

SPRINTS

A fast start is important in track racing and equally so in kayak racing. Line three or four boats up at one end of the pool and start them off at a given signal to sprint almost the entire length of the pool. The sprinting should be backwards as well as forwards, and even sideways using Sculling and Draw strokes.

SEQUENCES

One of the most popular ways to train for slalom is to design a course through several gates. The leader makes a demonstration run while the other boaters watch and try to memorize the course. Then, by starting a couple of boats only 10 seconds or so apart, it is possible to maintain two racers on the course at a time—always under the relentless hand of the stopwatch.

Backward paddling, especially through a gate, is an art often neglected. Entire sequences can be designed in which all the gates are negotiated in reverse, one after another. To add a little spice throw in an Eskimo Roll or two as well.

EXERGENIE CONTEST

An exergenie provides extra drag against which the boater must paddle. It is a small metal tube through which you thread a rope, twisting the rope inside: the amount of twist determines the degree of resistance. Exergenies are for sale in sport shops.

Thread a nylon rope as long as the pool through the exergenie and fasten one end of the rope to the stern grabloop of a kayak. At a signal, the boater springs forward, drawing the entire length of rope through the exergenie to the far end of the pool. When a boater has pulled the rope the length of the pool under a stopwatch several times, he is usually quite ready to suggest switching places with the timers. This exercise is best done with a fairly narrow-bladed paddle.

KAYAK POLO

Kayak polo, a favorite of the Ledyard Canoe Club, can be played in an indoor pool (2 boats per side) or outside in flatwater (3 or 4 boats per side) in either K–1's or C–1's. A good fast game builds stamina, increases paddling skills and maneuverability and is a worthwhile change from formal training.

Players use their paddles as mallets and try to hit a volley ball or water-polo ball into the opponent's goal (a loose net inside a rectangular frame about 3 feet above the water). Every boat should have a rubber tip on its bow, and players should wear helmets. Players cannot use hands or elbows to touch the ball, an opponent, or a boat.

OUTDOOR TRAINING

If you are fortunate enough to live near water with a moving current or rapids, you can have a lot of fun working out various practice routines to develop basic moves and skills during the warm-weather months. Most of the exercises and games recommended for pool training are just as effective outdoors, especially sequences, English Gates, sprints, the chase and, of course, kayak polo. Unless vandalism is a factor, or the sensitivities of fishermen are involved, you may be able to set up permanent gates on a river.

You don't need to have real rapids and lots of whitewater in your backyard in order to train outdoors. Check the topographic maps, visit the nearest dam. There is more whitewater around than you may think. You don't need much. The Czechoslovakian national whitewater team, for example, conducts much of its practice in moving current under a bridge right in the heart of the city of Prague.

Appendix

Whitewater Clubs

National Organizations

American Canoe Association
4260 E. Evans Avenue
Denver, CO 80222

Canadian Canoe Association
333 Vanier Road
Ottawa, Canada

American Whitewater Affiliation
East Side Drive
Concord, NH 03301

State and Local Clubs

Knik Kanoers and Kayakers
3014 Columbia
Anchorage, AK 99504

Aspen Kayak and Canoe Club
P.O. Box 1520
Aspen, CO 81611

Feather River Kayak Club
1773 Broadway Street
Marysville, CA 95901

Fibark Boat Races, Inc.
P.O. Box 762
Salida, CO 81201

Colorado Whitewater Association
1400 Dayton Street
Aurora, CO 80010

Georgia Canoeing Association
P.O. Box 7023
Atlanta, GA 30305

Sawtooth Wildwater Club
1255 Elm Street
Mountain Home, ID 83647

Belleville Whitewater Club
No. 3 Oakwood
Belleville, IL 62223

Chicago Whitewater Association
5652 S. California
Chicago, IL 60629

Kekionga Voyageurs
1818 Kensington Boulevard
Fort Wayne, IN 46805

Johnson County Canoe Club
7832 Rosewood Lane
Prairie Village, KS 66208

The Viking Canoe Club
3108 Rodaway Drive
Louisville, KY 40216

Bayou Haystackers
624 Moss Street
New Orleans, LA 70119

Bates Outing Club
Bates College
Lewiston, ME 04240

Penobscot Paddle and Chowder
Society
P.O. Box 121
Stillwater, ME 04489

Appalachian River Runners
Federation
P.O. Box 107
McHenry, MD 21541

Canoe Cruisers Association
6827 Red Top Road No. 1–B
Takoma Park, MD 20012

Hampshire College Outdoors
Program
Amherst, MA 01002

Appalachian Mountain Club
3 Joy Street
Boston, MA 02108

Cochituate Canoe Club
99 Dudley Road
Cochituate, MA 01760

Raw Strength and Courage
Kayakers
2022 Day Street
Ann Arbor, MI 48104

Minnesota Canoe Association
P.O. Box 14177, Union Station
Minneapolis, MN 55414

Ozark Wilderness Waterways Club
6729 Kenwood Avenue
Kansas City, MO 64131

Montana Kayak Club
P.O. Box 213
Brady, MT 59416

Ledyard Canoe Club
Robinson Hall
Hanover, NH 03755

Androscoggin Canoe and Kayak
Club
Lancaster, NH 03584

Kayak and Canoe Club of New
York
6 Winslow Avenue
East Brunswick, NJ 08816

Albuquerque Whitewater Club
804 Warm Sands Drive S.E.
Albuquerque, NM 87123

Niagara Gorge Kayak Club
41–17th Street
Buffalo, NY 14213

Nantahala Outdoor Center
Star Route Box 68
Bryson City, NC 28713

Mr. Canoe
425 Anthony Wayne Trail
#214
Waterville, OH 43566

Oregon Kayak and Canoe Club
P.O. Box 692
Portland, OR 97205

Wildwater Boating Club
Lock Box 179
Bellefonte, PA 16823

Philadelphia Canoe Club
4900 Ridge Avenue
Philadelphia, PA 19128

Penn State Outing Club
118 South Buckhout Street
State College, PA 16801

Scudder Falls Wildwater Club
795 River Road
Yardley, PA 19067

Rhode Island River Rats
53 Maplewood Avenue
Misquamicut, RI 02891

Brown University Outing Club
Providence, RI 02912

Carolina Whitewater Canoeing
Association
3142 Harvard Avenue
Columbia, SC 29205

East Tennessee Whitewater Club
P.O. Box 3074
Oak Ridge, TN 37830

Down River Club—Dallas
1412 Oak Lea
Irving, TX 75063

Johnson State Outing Club
Johnson State College
Johnson, VT 05656

Washington Kayak Club
8519 California Avenue, S.W.
Seattle, WA 98116

Whitewater Northwest Kayak Club
P.O. Box 1081
Spokane, WA 99201

West Virginia Wildwater
Association
Rt. 1 Box 97
Ravenswood, WV 26164

Wisconsin Hoofers Outing Club
1309 West Dayton
Madison, WI 53715

Ontario Voyageurs Kayak Club
365 Markham Street
Toronto 174 Ontario
Canada

British Columbia Kayak and
Canoe Club
1606 West Broadway
Vancouver, British Columbia
Canada

Manufacturers and Distributors

This list attempts to be complete, but because many whitewater manufacturers are small businesses, new ones come and old ones go with some frequency. We apologize for any errors. Most of the manufacturers listed will be happy to supply literature and refer you to the nearest retailer of their product. Some will accept mail orders. It should be noted that ordering boats by mail is difficult because of their size and consequently high shipping costs. The reference to canoes on this list means C–1 and/or C–2, not open canoes.

Baldwin Boat Co., RFD 2, Box 141, Orrington, ME 04474. Fiberglass kayaks, canoes, sailboats.

Bart Hauthaway, 640 Boston Post Road, Weston, MA 02193. Boats, paddles, equipment.

Cannon Products, 2345 N.E. 8th Ave., Faribault, MN 55021. Paddles.

Easy Rider Fiberglass Boat Co., 10013 51st Ave. SW, Seattle, WA 98146. Fiberglass kayaks and canoes, paddles, accessories. Catalogue. Licensee for Paul Hahn boat designs.

Foldbot Corp., Stark Industrial Park, Charleston, SC 29405. Folding and rigid canvas/wood kayaks; fiberglass kayaks. Kits, paddles, accessories.

Hyperform, 25 E. Industrial Park Rd., Hingham, MA 02043. Fiberglass kayaks and canoes, paddles, accessories. Licensee for Toni Prijon and Klaus Lettmann boat designs.

Illiad, Inc., 168 Circuit St., Norwell, MA 02061. Fiberglass kayak and canoe paddles.

Mad River Canoes and Kayaks by Tubbs, P.O. Box 363, Spring Hill, Waitsfield, VT 05673. Fiberglass canoes and kayaks and kits.

Millbrook Boats, Waitsfield, VT 05673. Fiberglass canoe specialist.

Old Town Canoe Co., Old Town, ME 04468. Fiberglass kayaks and canoes. ABS kayaks. Paddles, accessories.

Phoenix Products, Inc., Rt. 421, Tyner, KY 40486. Fiberglass kayaks, paddles, equipment.

Rapidesigns, Inc., 1296 Lowell Rd., Schenectady, NY 12308. Fiberglass kayaks.

Seda Products, P.O. Box 5509, Fullerton, CA 92635. Fiberglass kayaks, canoes, paddles, accessories.

Tubbs of Vermont, Forest Dale, VT 05745. Fiberglass kayaks.

Whitewater West, 727 S. 33rd St., Richmond, CA 94804. Fiberglass kayaks and canoes, paddles, accessories.

Wildwater Designs, Charles C. Walbridge, Penllyn Pike and Morris Road, Penllyn, PA 19422. Wet-suit, lifejacket, spray-skirt kits.

Importers

Eastern Mountain Sports, 1041 Commonwealth Ave., Boston, MA 02215. Also locations in Amherst, MA; North Conway, NH; Ardsley, NY. Fiberglass kayaks and canoes. Also domestically produced kayaks and canoes. Paddles, accessories.

Hans Klepper Corp., 35 Union Square West, New York, NY 10003. Folding kayaks, paddles, accessories. Fiberglass kayaks.

Tyne Kayaks, Dept. 69, 14 Alpha Road, Chelmsford, MA 01824.

Water Meister Sports, P.O. Box 5026, Fort Wayne, IN 46805.

Index

NOTE: *Unless specified otherwise, all entries apply primarily to kayaks and kayaking.*